a Gift for

_____

From

_____

How Great Our *Joy*

BROADMAN & HOLMAN PUBLISHERS • NASHVILLE, TENNESSEE

Contents

Introduction

It's Thanksgiving evening. About fifteen Ortlund family members are crowded into daughter Margie and John's living room. We're all more stuffed than the turkey was earlier, and everybody's mellowed out.

Then suddenly Margie cries, "Is Thanksgiving over yet?"

We all shout, "Yes!" (We do it every year; it's a family tradition thing.)

And Margie bellows, *"Merry Christmas!"* while simultaneously starting Christmas music on the stereo. With that, for the Ortlunds, the Christmas season has begun for another year.

And we say to you as you pick up this book: This is a new time for you, too.

You've never lived this Christmas before.

You're at a new place in your life. So much has happened to you since last Christmas!

Sure, the truths of Christmas aren't new; they were established before the foundation of the world. The story of Christmas itself is two thousand years old.

But for you and us, this Christmas season is brand new.

So be blessed by this book. Be deepened. Keep praising.

Have a merry, most joyful Christmas!

Part One

Don't Forget the Joy!

In the same region, shepherds were living out in the fields and keeping watch at night over their flock. Then an angel of the Lord stood before them . . . and they were terrified. But the angel said to them, "Do not be afraid, for you see, I announce to you good news of great joy that will be for all the people: because today in the city of David was born for you a Savior, who is Christ the Lord." *Luke 2:8–11*

What will occupy you most this Christmas season:

burdens or Joys?

The shepherds that first Christmas night were probably burdened . . . with all the usual culprits: straying lambs, wool ticks, cut hooves, nighttime cold.

Then suddenly they were exposed to angels, international news, and glory—*brilliant, radiant,*

Shekinah Glory!

They could never be the same again.

The shepherds returned *"glorifying and praising God for all they had seen and heard"* (Luke 2:20). Sure, they returned to wool ticks and cut hooves, but forever after they would see all their annoyances through new eyes.

Christian, are you burdened with the "usual"?

You, too, have been exposed to all the splendor, all the joy, all the majesty of God's eternal plans, set in motion by the birth of Jesus.

Then don't be absorbed by the burdens! Do your daily work this Christmas *glorifying and praising God for all you have seen and heard.*

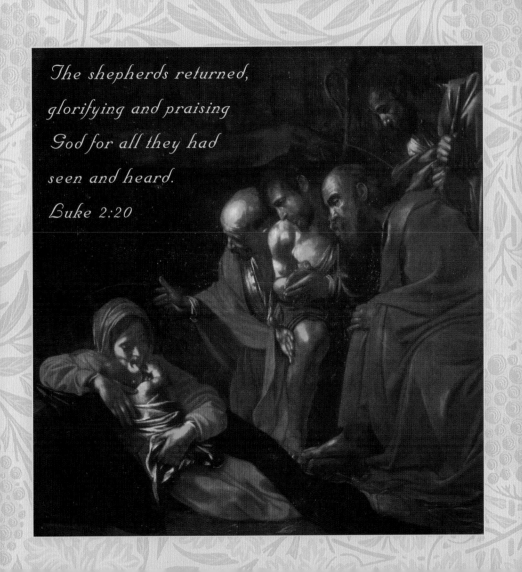

The shepherds returned, glorifying and praising God for all they had seen and heard.

Luke 2:20

Oh, ring Noel,
Each loud Christmas bell;
God's good news is great news
all over the earth!
And Christians—all sing it
As bells ring and ring it;
Applaud it and laud it,
this wonderful birth!
Yes, ring it out, fling it out,
chiming and clanging:
On this joyous morn
Our Redeemer is born!

Can the world celebrate something it doesn't understand?

People of this world string their Christmas lights, not fully realizing that their decorations are saying to believers, *"Arise, shine, for your light has come, and the glory of the LORD rises upon you"* (Isaiah 60:1, NIV). They punch in their CDs that sing, "Oh, come let us adore Him, Christ the Lord!"

Matthew 13:13,16 says, *"Looking they do not see, and hearing they do not listen or understand. . . . But your eyes are blessed because they do see, and your ears because they do hear!"*

So this holiday season, don't be a Scrooge. Don't grumble over the commercialization of Christmas. *Blessed are your eyes and ears that can comprehend what all this beauty really means.*

Do the sights and sounds of Christmas draw you a little higher?

Drink in. Cherish it. Rejoice! And pray that some who have lived in the dark all year long will find the Light of the world in the lights of Christmas.

At this new Christmas season, worship Him. Between your ears, within your heart, where no one sees but God alone — worship Him!

Often confess your sins to Him. Often think on His characteristics. From moment to moment, as much as you're able, keep a running conversation going with your Father.

He will love it.

Worship Him

As you move through the Christmas lights
and beauty, worship Him.

As you write your cards, worship Him.

As you trim your tree, worship Him.

As you spend, be spent.

As you serve others, serve Him.

Let your heart keep welling up with
"glory to God in the highest!"

What joy the Christ of Christmas brings,

And life and peace and all good things!

Be full, our friends,

Filled to the brim;

Be full of joy,

Be full of Him.

Could you use a fill-up in your joy compartment?

When Elizabeth, the mother of John the Baptist, *"was filled with the Holy Spirit . . . she exclaimed with a loud cry: 'Blessed are you among women, and blessed is your offspring!'"* (Luke 1:41,42).

When her husband Zechariah *"was filled with the Holy Spirit,"* he prophesied, *"Blessed is the Lord"* (Luke 1:67,68).

Even their baby, John, was *"filled with the Holy Spirit while still in his mother's womb"* (Luke 1:15). And when he grew up, he went everywhere preaching as *"a voice of one crying out in the wilderness"* (Luke 3:4).

Be filled with the *Holy Spirit!*

Mary, after the most amazing of all fillings of the Holy Spirit, exclaimed, *"My soul proclaims the greatness of the Lord. . . . Holy is His name"* (Luke 1:46,49).

Pick up the Christmas tradition started by these early ones. They were all filled with the Holy Spirit, and they opened their mouths in joyful praise.

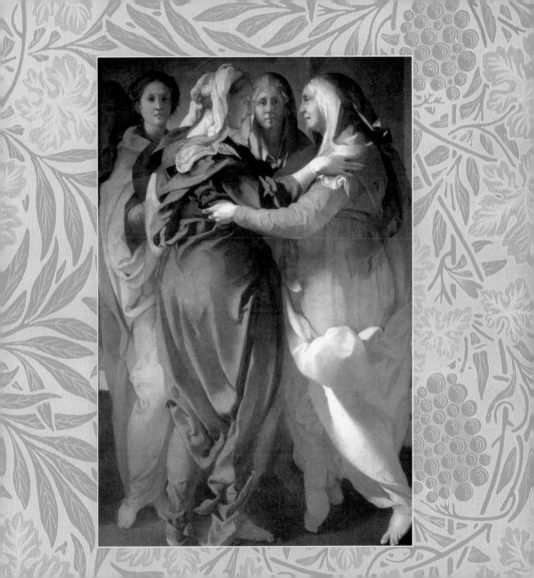

Family Reflections

We're gathered around the table after Christmas dinner, and I, the matriarch of the Ortlund tribe, ask the family a question:

"Do you know what the four stages of life are? Stage one: you believe in Santa Claus. Stage two: you don't believe in Santa Claus. Stage three: you are Santa Claus. Stage four: you look like Santa Claus!"

Everybody guffaws.

The pushed-back, peaceful moments after Christmas dinner are a time when we always contribute our silly holiday humor; it's another family tradition.

Firstborn Sherry pipes up (I'll identify each one: husband Walt Harrah writes, arranges, sings, and produces Christian music): "Have you heard this one? A Russian named Rudolph looks out the window to check the weather. 'It's raining,' he says. But his wife replies, 'No, I think that's snow.' 'It's rain,' says Rudolph. 'Snow,' says his wife. Finally, Rudolph ends the debate once and for all: "Rudolph the Red knows rain, dear.' "

Loud Ortlund groans.

We also pass out silly Christmas greeting cards; everybody's brought a few. (We bring silly cards to our family birthday parties, too.) Second-born Margie (husband John McClure is a pastor in Newport Beach) has deviated from tradition.

She's brought a Hanukkah card: Moses is on the mountain, kneeling in front of the two completed tablets of the law. He looks up and says, "Lord, we've got a little extra space here at the bottom. Want to put something about brushing after meals?"

Ray, Jr. (a pastor in Augusta, Georgia) throws his head back and laughs so hard he cackles, and pretty soon everybody's laughing at Ray laughing.

Fourth child Nels (a policeman in Monrovia, California) has forgotten his cards, but off-the-cuff he contributes something else: "Did you hear about the traveling salesman who saw a three-legged chicken run across the road in front of him and into a farmyard? Well, he couldn't resist. He stopped his car and said to the farmer, 'Hey, do you know you've got a chicken with three legs?' 'Yeah, all our chickens got three legs,' said the farmer. 'We done bred 'em that way.' 'Why?' asked the salesman. 'Because folks like extra drumsticks.' The salesman was amazed. 'How do they taste?' he asked. 'We don't know,' said the farmer. 'We ain't never been able to catch one!' "

"That has nothing to do with Christmas!" we all howl. Then we pelt him with wadded-up, used Christmas wrappings until he's pretty much buried.

Enjoy!

Enjoy the Christ of Christmas!

Enjoy the ones you love!

For "every good and perfect gift

Cometh from above."

Have you heard what the angels are saying?

Several times in history, God has poked a hole through the sky and let His divine joy shine down on us.

When Solomon first dedicated God's temple, fire came down from heaven and consumed the burnt offerings, and the priests couldn't go inside the temple because the glory of the Lord had filled it like a cloud.

And at the first Christmas, when God's Son arrived, He sent a vast array of angels singing thrilling songs, as well as a very special, shining, mystical star. God pulled out the stops!

The words of the angels' song recorded in Luke 2:14 were full of joy: *"Glory to God in the highest heaven, and peace on earth to people He favors!"*

Have you forgotten where you left your joy?

Jesus' first coming to earth can still result in glory to God and peace on earth. That's revival, renewal!

The two of us have seen it happen over and over, as God's people in missions groups or churches—dry, tired, bugged at each other—have experienced His Spirit's cleansing and refreshing. Invariably, their faces shine with a renewed sense of glory to God, and their hearts swell with a desire for restored peace among men.

And then—oh, how they sing!

Could you use a little of that right now?

Tell Him today. *And don't forget the joy!*

Joy!

Try to catch the scope of their song:

Those in the highest places in heaven
eternally enjoy His glory.

Those on earth—through all ages
of human history—can enjoy His peace.

All heaven and earth are deeply affected
with joy by the birth of Christ.

For you and us another year has fled,

And varied are the ways that God has led.

But if the year brought stress to you,

Or loss,

Christ came to bear them all

Upon His cross.

So Christmas joy is deep

And good

And strong.

Look up, our friend,

And sing a Christmas song!

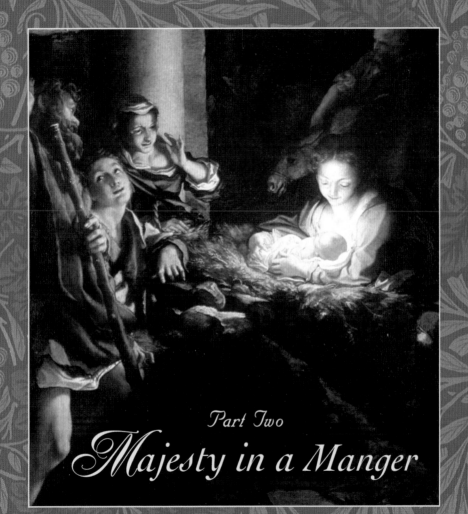

Part Two
Majesty in a Manger

This will be a sign for you: you will find a baby

wrapped snugly in cloth and lying in a manger.

Luke 2:12

Consider how

His star shone down,

Revealing cradle,

Cross,

And crown.

"Lift up your heads, O you gates!

Be lifted up, you ancient doors,

That the King of glory may come in!"

(Psalm 24:7, NIV)

That Christmas day the King came in!

He pushed our hearts' doors open wide

(So long closed up by pain and sin)

and strode inside.

"Who is this King of glory?"
"The LORD strong and mighty,
The LORD mighty in battle"

(Psalm 24:8, NIV)

But, oh, You came so meek and soft,

Surprising us with baby form

And stars and song and cattle loft and hay so warm.

Our King of Glory!

How can we express

The wonder of your power and graciousness?

What made Christ's coming unlike any other,
unlike any since?

A number of "comings" in secular history had awesome effects on their day. Napoleon, for example, in 1815. The year before, he had been banished from France to Elba, and it looked as if that were the end of Napoleon.

But even while separated from his homeland, he had been keeping up with events. In March 1815—barely a year after his exile—having gotten word about how weak and unpopular his successor (Louis XVIII) was, and knowing that the common people of France still wished for him, Napoleon went back to France.

The emperor heard that Napoleon had returned, and he sent a whole army out to capture him. As the army advanced toward him, Napoleon got out of his carriage and started walking toward the oncoming troops. He was alone; he was defenseless. He just walked right toward them! And when he got close enough, he opened his coat, so that if they chose to fire they could aim right at his heart. And he said quietly, "Frenchmen, it's your emperor."

The soldiers went wild. They kissed his hands. They fell at his feet. They picked him up and carried him on their shoulders, and they roared at the top of their lungs, "Long live the Emperor! Long live the Emperor!"

Two thousand years ago, a much greater King came among the people—and His coming was even quieter, humbler, and more vulnerable.

Here's how Luke 2 describes it:

"While [Joseph and Mary] were [in Bethlehem], it happened that the days were completed for her to give birth. Then she gave birth to her firstborn Son, and she wrapped Him snugly in cloth and laid Him in a manger—because there was no room for them at the inn."

Hebrews 10:5-7 describes it in a larger perspective:

"As He was coming into the world, He said: . . . You prepared a body for Me. . . . I have come . . . to do your will, O God!"

Titus 3:4–5 steps back still farther, picturing Christ's coming in maybe the most awesome way of all: *"When the goodness and love for man appeared from God our Savior, He saved us."*

Like Napoleon, but far vaster in scope, Christ arrived, saying, "My children, it's your Savior."

What a coming!

Come...

Christ has come to you.

Now you come to Him.

Come humbly, as the shepherds did.

Come bringing gifts, as the wise men did.

But come!

O come, dear friend,

to the Christmas Child,

To a Baby soft with His

Head laid down.

Oh, kneel at His crib.

When you lift your eyes,

A Man from a cross

Will have cleft the skies,

And His head will shine

With a dazzling crown!

What if Christ had not come that first Christmas?

For one thing, the world would still be caught in the death-hold of slavery. When Christ was born, three out of every five humans were slaves. The clanking of chains could be heard everywhere. Roman law said that if you killed someone's ox, you paid for it with your own life. But if you killed a slave — no problem!

But, oh, the coming of Christ rang the deathknell of slavery! Even today as His principles are taught, slavery shrinks and disappears. One day it will be gone altogether.

If Christ had not come, women everywhere would still be used and abused. When Christ was born, women were considered inconsequential and a burden, good only for their ability to produce children and for the contributions of their toil and work.

But Jesus was a champion of women! They were some of His dearest friends. Women were the last to be with Him at His death and the first to see Him at His resurrection. And through the centuries since, when His principles are upheld, women acquire a place of dignity, honor, and worth in society.

Jesus touched lepers, loved the poor, held children on His lap, comforted widows, and healed the sick. He told us what things are important — not "things" but people. *"What is a man benefited,"* He challenged us, *"if he gains the whole world, yet loses or forfeits himself?"* (Luke 9:25).

And ever since, the truest test of any civilization's worth isn't the skyscrapers it builds or the accumulation of wealth or technology it produces, but rather the way it cares for its weakest, poorest, and most vulnerable. Stocks won't last; crops won't last; computer chips won't last; but the least human beings will last for all eternity.

In Matthew 13, He called us a treasure.

In Luke 15, He compared us to sheep and promised that the Good Shepherd would go through anything to find even one of us that gets lost!

If Christ hadn't come, we'd have never understood
the preciousness of one soul —
the preciousness of you, our friend —
in the sight of God.

When Christ was born on Christmas morn,

A dream was born of infinite care

That you and I would find a cross —

And meet Him there.

When Christ was born on Christmas morn,

A dream was born of glorious worth,

That wolves and lambs would dwell in peace

And latter rains make crops increase

On all the earth.

When Christ was born on Christmas morn,

A dream was born — God's own great scheme

That sin and death would soon be past

And kingdom peace emerge at last.

Oh, friend, be glad!

Look up! Hold fast

the
*Christmas
Dream!*

When Jesus was born…

    The present heavens knew their end was near—

When the stars would drop like shriveled figs,

    The sky be rolled up like an old parchment scroll,

        And the sun and moon be replaced by

            The Lord, our Light.

When Jesus was born…

    The present earth knew it was terminal.

A new one would emerge

    Where wolves, lambs, lions, and oxen all browse together,

        And snakes eat dust, and dust only,

    And nothing will hurt or destroy

        On all God's holy mountain.

When Jesus was born...

Weakness was condemned to death,
And so was death itself, and waste and sickness
And frustration and alarm and fatigue,
And insensitivity, complacency, mediocrity, deceit,
Greed, laziness, egocentricity, and all the rest.

When Jesus was born...

So was hope!
The way was paved for the Kingdom, when all our
Inventing, organizing, creating, producing, and
Tweaking will be uninhibited!
And we'll plant with expectation and reap with joy!
And a thousand, thousand dreams will come true.

Think about what Jesus started,
And have a Merry Christmas!

What do you name a baby who was sent to save the world?

Hear the angel's message from God the Father to Joseph:

"[Mary] will give birth to a son, and you are to name Him Jesus, because He will save His people from their sins" (Matthew 1:21).

Yet the Bible also gives many other names of Jesus to explain the wonder and majesty of His person. He is Light, Life, the Word, the Alpha and Omega, the Head of the body, the Ancient of Days, and plenty more. But His most loved name, His Christmas name—Jesus—is the key to understanding all the others.

Interestingly, none of His disciples are recorded as calling Him "Jesus" to His face. They called Him "Lord," "Master," "Teacher," "Rabbi," but they never addressed Him as "Jesus."

Maybe they felt His name was too sacred to use in His presence. Only later would they write of Him as "Jesus" or "Lord Jesus" or "the Lord Jesus Christ."

They understood that there was power in that name.

Peter said to a lame man, *"I have neither silver nor gold, but what I have, I give to you: In the name of Jesus Christ the Nazarene, get up and walk! . . . So [the man] jumped up, stood, and started to walk"* (Acts 3:6,8).

No wonder Paul lifted up that name and wrote, "At the name of Jesus every knee should bow—of those who are in heaven and on earth and under the earth" (Philippians 2:10).

Our friend—love and honor His Christmas name! Speak it with care. Believe what it means, and call His name *"Jesus, because He will save His people from their sins."*

The word "He" in that sentence is placed in the emphatic position, meaning that He and He alone would save His people.

"There is salvation in no one else, for there is no other name under heaven given to people by which we must be saved" (Acts 4:12).

He and He alone, all by Himself, would purge away our sins. And none of His saving work would be left undone! He began the saving; He continued it; and He finished it. Jesus is the perfect, complete Savior.

"He will save his people from their sins."

If what we needed most was a philosopher or a political leader, God would have sent His Son to be that. But what we needed most was a Savior from our sins. And—praise God— we have one.

His
name
is *Jesus*

Praise the Lord from the heavens!

Praise Him, all you heavenly hosts,

Sun and moon and shining stars!

Praise the Lord from the earth!

Great sea creatures, ocean depths,

Mountains and all hills,

Trees, wild animals, cattle!

Praise Him, magi and shepherds—all flesh!

Praise Him in holy Christmas joy!

The Center of the Center

Is a tiny Boy,

And all the universe

His creche.

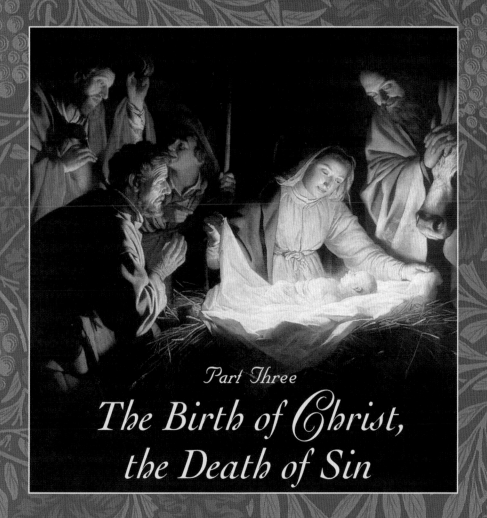

Part Three

The Birth of Christ, the Death of Sin

"Indeed, this child is destined to cause the fall and rise of many in Israel, and to be a sign that will be opposed— and a sword will pierce your own soul—that the thoughts of many hearts may be revealed."

Luke 2:34–35

Christmas was planned before winters or springs,

    Before lions had paws, before sparrows had wings.

But then came Creation—and rabbits and fish

    And donkeys and people; they all wished one wish:

"We wish that we weren't so afraid of each other,

    That folks wouldn't quarrel or brother hate brother!"

Then finally came Christmas:

    The Word was made flesh,

And dear Baby Jesus was laid in a creche.

Sleep, Baby, sleep: The Kingdom will come.

    Lions, rabbits—be of good cheer!

Sing, angels, sing—no longer be dumb;

    Tell the great story:

        The Savior is here!

Family Reflections

It was the week before Christmas in Pasadena, California. Ray was pastor of the Lake Avenue Congregational Church there, so he was a little bit known. Or did this phone call come from somebody's looking in the Yellow Pages?

Anyway, we got a call from (of all places) Los Angeles' Juvenile Hall, part of the city's correctional facilities. *Would our family come give them a program on Christmas morning?*

We quickly commenced a group powwow. "It could be our family's Christmas present to Jesus," Ray said. So we agreed. While I played the piano, Ray and the children would sing a "special Christmas number." Then each of us would share something from a Christmas Scripture verse: I, Sherry, Margie, Ray, Jr., Bud—they were all high schoolers. Then Dad would preach.

Early Christmas morning (no presents yet, not even stocking gifts) we dressed and drove to downtown L.A. and parked in the cold, gray parking lot of this giant, cold, gray building. A series of cold, gray doors opened for us and clanged shut behind us, and we were ushered into a huge, cold, gray assembly hall.

Soon a few hundred boys filed in, from little ones through the teen years, shepherded by plenty of guards. They noisily piled into their chairs, heads down, looking so defeated, so despondent! Christmas morning—and they were so far from home . . . (if they had homes)! We "did our thing" with aching hearts, and then the boys filed out.

In a few minutes a few hundred girls came spilling in, again accompanied by those ever-present guards, and they, too, noisily piled into the chairs with their heads down and eyes averted. I groaned a wordless prayer: "Oh, Lord—"

Before our turn came, a girls' choir filed across the front and began to sway and sing "Sweet Little Jesus Boy," cuddled in tender, soft rock. Christmas morning! It was too much. A girl in the crowd began to cry—out loud! Another girl began to cry. Another began to wail— girls in jail on Christmas, realizing how badly they'd blown it because "they didn't know who [He] was." Soon they were all wailing, and the wailing grew louder into an anguished roar, a sustained scream! The large hall nearly burst with the deafening reverberations.

It was over almost before it started. The guards led the girls out. The choir number never got finished. We didn't sing; we didn't speak; Ray didn't even preach. The guards escorted us out of the cold, gray assembly hall, through the same series of cold, gray doors clanging shut behind us, and out into the cold, gray parking lot. We drove home.

Oh, the pain of sin!

Long time before, old Simeon had prophesied to Mary: *"Indeed, this child is destined to cause the fall and rise of many . . . and to be a sign that will be opposed—and a sword will pierce your own soul—that the thoughts of many hearts may be revealed"* (Luke 2:34,35).

Christmas ushered in the eventual falling of many people:

Nero. Hitler. Stalin.

Us. You.

The teenagers in Juvenile Hall.

Everybody.

We all have fallen.

"There is no one righteous, not even one. . . . All have turned away, together they have become useless" (Romans 3:10,12). Even *"all our righteous acts are like filthy rags"* (Isaiah 64:6, NIV)

And this Christmas Child Himself, when He was grown, said, *"The Father, in fact, judges no one but has given all judgment to the Son. . . . He has granted Him the right to pass judgment, because He is the Son of Man"* (John 5:22,27).

So this Child was destined to be the Great and Final Judge, when *"the thoughts of many hearts [will] be revealed."*

BUT—it would be too heart-stopping, too anguishing, too terrible to contemplate if this Child had not also been destined to cause the rising of many!

"Who is this?" asked Isaiah many centuries before Jesus was born, *"robed in splendor, striding forward in the greatness of his strength?"*

And the Eternal Christ Himself answered, *"It is I, speaking in righteousness, mighty to save."*

"Why are your garments red," the prophet asked, *"like those of one treading the winepress?"*

"I have trodden the winepress alone. . . . There was no one to help . . . so my own arm worked salvation for me" (Isaiah 63:1-3,5, NIV).

So, *"When the completion of the time came, God sent His Son, born of a woman"* (Galatians 4:4).

And the Christmas angel told Joseph, *"You are to name Him Jesus, because He will save His people from their sins"* (Matthew 1:21).

What if we told you the most expensive gift was for you?

There's a deep, rumbling, groaning echo of sadness when we think about what it meant for God the Father to send His Son from heaven. John 3:17 gives us a hint of this: *"For God did not send His Son into the world that He might judge the world, but that the world might be saved through Him."*

The original Greek word "send" could be translated, "He did not *send off* his Son into the world." When Christ was "sent off," it meant separation between the Father and His beloved Son. He "sent Him off" to save the world, the verse says, and yet the Father knew that the world would thank Him for His act of loving mercy by buffeting the Son, abusing Him, murdering Him. Can you imagine how the Father had to feel, when He "sent off" His lovely Son?

One of the most loved of all Scriptures is John 3:16: *"For God loved the world in this way: He gave His only Son, so that everyone who believes in Him will not perish but have eternal life."*

God emptied heaven! None was so precious to Him as His only Son, yet He gave Him. But, friends, the sacrifice began long before the cross, and it was a sacrifice full of emotion. There was joy in knowing the ultimate victory of the resurrection, yet there was also deep grief.

Don't take lightly the cost of Christmas to God the Father. Love was behind it all. Love was the reason—the only reason— that Almighty God was willing to pay such a dreadful price.

And don't take lightly the cost of Christmas to Christ the Son. John writes, *"In the beginning was the Word; and the Word was with God, and the Word was God"* (John 1:1). The original Greek word "with" could be translated "the Son was facing the Father." It implies a deep intimacy between Them in all the pasts of eternity. Before there was our universe, there was the Holy Trinity.

Jesus, just before His cross, commented on the glory of this fellowship: *"Now, Father, glorify Me in your presence with that glory I had with You before the world existed"* (John 17:5). A splendor — a radiance — had existed in the Father-Son relationship which, at the first Christmas, necessarily had to change. For thirty-three years, They would both miss it.

Second Corinthians 8:9 gives us this tender explanation of the cost of Christmas to Jesus: *"For you know the grace of our Lord Jesus Christ: although He was rich, for your sake He became poor, so that by His poverty you might become rich."*

"By His poverty!" How poor did Christ become?

First, our glorious Second Person of the Godhead became a baby—a vulnerable, human baby—dependent on Joseph and Mary to feed and clothe and protect Him. A baby has nothing.

Second, He grew up as a "nobody," a man *"of no reputation"* (Philippians 2:7, KJV). Throughout eternity past, all heaven had adored and worshiped Him. Suddenly on earth, His true identity was unknown; His claims were discounted. People even called Him a blasphemer or (worse) a demoniac!

Third, He was nailed to a cross, bearing all the sin of the world, and rejected completely by His own, beloved, eternal Abba.

Oh, the cost of Christmas to Christ the Son! Don't take it lightly!

And yet He endured it all *"for the joy that lay before Him"* (Hebrews 12:2). The joy of making you rich! The joy of forgiving your sins and reconciling you to the Father! The joy of providing you with access to the riches of God's glory through prayer! The joy of giving you a loving family of God! The joy of opening for you the doors of heaven and lavishing on you His love and care until you get there!

Praise God for Christmas! Praise God that He was willing to pay the cost—every last penny of it! Praise God for His incredible grace! It truly is, for us . . .

Great Riches At Christ's Expense!

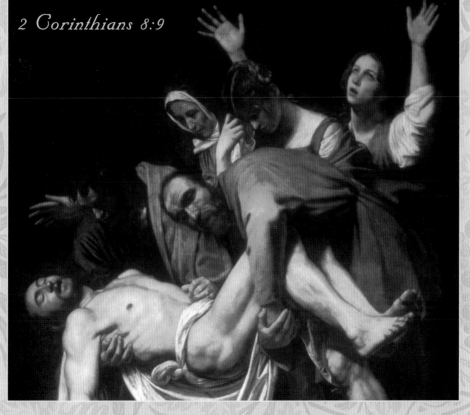

For you know the grace of our Lord Jesus Christ: although He was rich, for your sake He became poor, so that by His poverty you might become rich.

2 Corinthians 8:9

The Spirit brooded,

Brooded over dawn's creation

Till life and breath invaded everything,

And cows began to calve, and birds to sing,

And Adam grew to be a mighty nation.

The Spirit brooded,

Brooded over humble Mary —

That little maid, the overshadowed one —

Till He who formed in her was God's great Son,

The eternal Christ,

And she, His sanctuary.

Please, Spirit, brood—

Oh, brood upon Your waiting people!

Look down on groaning earth and groaning men;

Revive us, shake us, wake us!

Brood again—till glory lights our land,

And every tree's a steeple!

Got anything under that tree for the pain in our heels?

Listen carefully to the story of Christmas, and you can hear in the background the quiet, sinister hiss of a serpent. In fact, a writhing snake tail whipped about the heels of ancient history, trying its best to topple the whole event.

"S-s-s-s," the serpent breathed to Eve long before the first Christmas morn, and she ate the forbidden fruit and gave some to her husband, too.

But—(this is amazing!)—along with His punishments for Adam and Eve's sin, God simultaneously showed His incredible mercy and tender love, and He gave them (and us) this incredible hope: The woman's offspring, Jesus Christ, would ultimately crush Satan's head with a finishing blow, though the serpent would continue to strike the offspring's heel — painful punches, but not mortal blows (Genesis 3:15).

Through succeeding centuries the serpent kept striking and striking, trying to cut off the Christ to come.

"S-s-s-s," he breathed to Egypt's Pharaoh, who tried in Exodus 1 to murder all Jewish boy babies. He failed.

"S-s-s-s," he breathed again to Persia's King Xerxes, who tried in Esther 3 to wipe out all the Jews. The plot was aborted.

"S-s-s-s," he breathed in a last-ditch effort to Judea's King Herod, who tried in Matthew 2 to kill all Hebrew boy babies age two and under. But Joseph was warned in a dream and fled the country with his wife, Mary, and the universe's tiny new treasure, Jesus.

Ultimately, God's promise will prove true,
and Christ Jesus will triumph!

But for now, that first damaging blow inflicted on Adam and Eve has temporarily brought misery to all their descendants. *"Just as sin entered the world through one man, and death through sin, in this way death spread to all men, because all sinned"* (Romans 5:12).

Now, in a larger sense, the first couple's "offspring" includes all of us human beings. And ever since those two fell to the serpent's temptation, we've all known pain in our heels! *"The ancient serpent, who is called the Devil and Satan, the one who deceives the whole world"* (Revelation 12:9) continues to strike with his venomous bite, and we're all made miserable from it.

The two of us—Anne and Ray—are a microcosm of that. We are the "Adam and Eve" of our particular Ortlund tribe.

We were both raised carefully in godly homes where (to us) smoking a cigarette or going to a movie were unthinkable sins! But, still, the seeds of disobedience were alive and well within us both. In our early marriage, when some conflict would arise—

"S-s-s-s" could be heard hissing from somewhere in the house, and I, Anne, would get strong willed and accusatory, and I'd enflame the situation.

"S-s-s-s" would keep on breathing in the background, and I, Ray, would get defensive and hostile.

For within the two of us is every potential for every kind of evil. God (for His own mysterious reasons) has sheltered us from dysfunctional families and drugs and murders and prison sentences, but it's no credit to the two of us! Left to ourselves, we are easy prey for that "ancient serpent" that keeps writhing and striking our heels.

Even our offspring (now up to three generations, so far) deal with their own set of struggles against strong wills and defensiveness and every kind of misery! We bow our heads and know that the seeds of those things were within us, and when we bore children, we reproduced not only ourselves but also our sins.

Children, we are sorry! We repent a thousand times!

We apologize to you! Please forgive us.

But that first Christmas shouted loud and clear that the serpent was losing and that Christ would win. The reason Satan makes us all miserable, sometimes, is simply because he's a poor loser: *"For the Devil has come down to you with great fury, because he knows he has a short time"* (Revelation 12:12).

The Ortlund family celebrations—our gifts and songs and laughter and prayers—are not glib and superficial. We are tenderly aware of one another's depressions, battles, struggles, and miseries. We hold one another's hands and hug a lot, to get each other through.

Our heels hurt.

But those hurts, though painful, aren't ultimate. Christ, the victorious Christmas Child, is the ultimate One!

Soon He will crush Satan's head. And He shall save His people—including us—from our sins!

Cool!—as our kids would say.

Ye-ow!—as our grandkids would say.

Our great grandkids don't say nuthin'—yet.

But they will.

Oh, the beauty of the Christmas season,

Celebration of the Baby's birth!

Jesus Christ our Savior is the reason

Lights are glowing now around the earth.

May the light invade as well within,

Chasing out the dark of personal sin!

Holy,

Holy,

Holy is the Boy.

Holy be your peace; and pure, your joy.

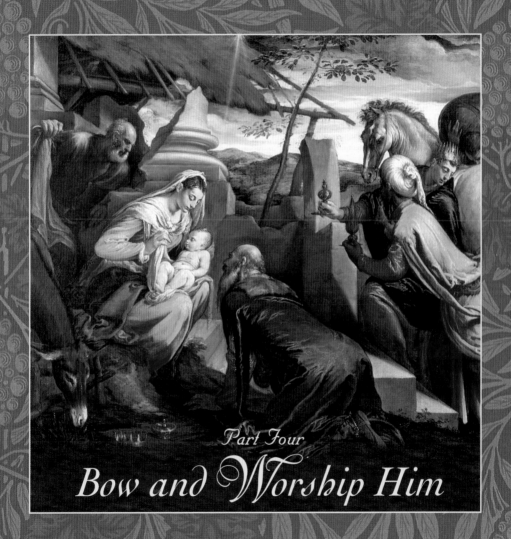

Part Four

Bow and Worship Him

They saw the child with Mary His mother,

and falling to their knees, they worshiped Him.

Matthew 2:11

Dear Christmas Jesus,
Tucked in your bed,
Cows at Your feet, Lord,
Lambs at Your head:
Say, did they know You,
There in the shed?

Whether they knew You
There in the stall,
Heaven has crowned You
King over all!

We, too, would know You,
Though we are small;
We want to love You,
Follow Your call.

How close have you come to giving up?

The first Christmas

happened because of Christ's surrendered will:

"As He was coming into the world, He said: 'You did not want sacrifice and offering, but You prepared a body for Me. . . . Then I said, 'See, I have come . . . to do Your will, O God!'" (Hebrews 10:5,7).

Calvary

happened because of Christ's surrendered will:

"He fell on His face, praying, 'My Father! If it is possible, let this cup pass from Me. Yet not as I will, but as You will'" (Matthew 26:39).

All God's magnificent purposes

—for your own life and for the entire flow of eternal history—

happen because of surrendered wills:

"Therefore, brothers, by the mercies of God, I urge you to present your

bodies as a living sacrifice, holy and pleasing to God . . . so that you may

discern what is the good, pleasing, and perfect will of God" (Romans 12:1,2).

How far can you trust an invisible God?

The virgin Mary—just a young girl—had a bold faith in a great God! What else could explain her total surrender to Him? When told she was going to give birth to the Son of God, her response was, *"Consider me the Lord's slave. . . . May it be done to me according to your word"* (Luke 1:38).

We might say, "Mary! What about Joseph? What's he going to think? And what will he do to you?" But Mary seems to say, "That's God's business. I rest in His ability to take care of me."

"What about the townspeople? What about the rumors?"

Calmly, evenly: "I trust the Lord about them, too."

Did Mary lose? No way. She is still honored and loved the world over. Friend, when you surrender to God's plan for your life, you never lose. That's not risky. In the long run, in fact, it's the only safe thing to do.

Surrender is foundational to life. The world says that surrender is not fair, that it's undemocratic. You might not get your rights, they say. You have to stay in control of your own life!

Oh, we promise you, that's the road to misery and failure. God loves you just as He loved Mary, and He will only do you good. Humble yourself, then, and tell Him (as she told the angel) *"May it be done to me according to your word."*

All over the world, when people humble themselves and surrender to God, they find a freedom and a future unlike any they could have manufactured through their own self-will.

Do yourself a big favor; you do the same.

What awesome news! In ancient stall
A Babe was born—too weak, too small
For most around to comprehend
How far His power would extend.

He is the Mighty God!

Give Him your praise,
Your frankincense and myrrh,
Your bended knee.
Give Him the joys and tears of all your days,
Your life,
Your soul,
Your strength,
Your piety.

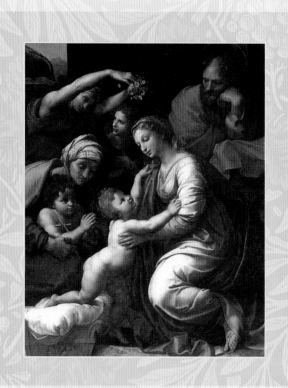

Here come people stealing, stealing
To the Christmas manger stall.
Oh, what wonder they are feeling —
Awe and wonder now revealing —
Hushed before the crib so small!

Those who come, come meekly,
weakly,
Those who come, come dumbly,
humbly,
Or they cannot come
at all.

Who is this baby—meek and mild?
Who is this humble Christmas child?

Humbling becomes us sinners. When God's Spirit is deeply at work in us, we humble ourselves (hard as it is to swallow our pride) and pray and seek His face and turn from our wicked ways—and God hears, forgives, and heals (2 Chronicles 7:14).

But why should Almighty God humble Himself? Here is the mystery of Christmas.

"Out of the ivory palaces

Into a world of woe;

Only His great, eternal love

Made my Savior go."

Christ had always, eternally, been alive and active. *"In the beginning was the Word,"* says John 1:1—and that reaches back before Genesis 1:1, before creation! Writes Frederick Bruehner,

> *"Just as His death was not the end of Him,*
> *So His birth was not the beginning of Him."*

He was Almighty God.

And yet He came into this world that first Christmas and *"emptied Himself by assuming the form of a slave, taking on the likeness of men"* (Philippians 2:7). Incredible! He created everything— and then He voluntarily submitted to His own creation.

Truly, profoundly, Christ Jesus humbled Himself.

O Christmas Child—
The Son of God, the Savior,
O tiny Babe—
Creation's Joy and Crown,
O Holy One—
The LORD of all forever:

We come before Your mercy seat,
Where wise men of the ages meet.
We lay our treasures at Your feet
And
bow
down.

Part Five

Immanuel Will Be with You

And remember,

I am with you always, to the end of the age.

Matthew 28:20

Could you boldly face the future if you knew God was with you?

"Now all this took place to fulfill what was spoken by the Lord through the prophet: 'See, the virgin will be with child and give birth to a son, and they will name Him Immanuel,' which is translated 'God is with us'" (Matthew 1:22–23).

"Immanuel." Let's take the name apart. The end "-el" is a name for God: "The Strong One." You see it in:

"Beth-el" (House of God),

"Ishma-el" (God will hear),

"Dani-el" (God the Judge), and so on.

And "Immanuel" means, "God, the Strong One, is with us."

"Immanuel" — "God with us"

But He's not "with us" to spy on us, to "get the scoop" on us, or condemn us. The Apostle Paul wrote that the Lord who is with us is also for us! Listen to Romans 8:31–32: *"If God is for us, who is against us? He did not even spare His own Son, but offered Him up for us all; how will He not also with Him grant us everything?"*

He came to us at Christmas and died for us at Calvary that He might be "with us"—here, now, and forever.

And when you believe that and receive Him, from then on He refuses to be without you, ever again.

A while back some missionaries were imprisoned in China, and they weren't allowed even to talk to each other. With time they grew hungry, cold, and discouraged. One had figured out a calendar system for keeping track of the days, and eventually he knew it was Christmas Day.

He fashioned letters from straw on the floor, and—without the guards noticing—put together the word "IMMANUEL."

When the light of understanding dawned on the other prisoners' faces, suddenly it seemed as if that miserable cell began to glow with Christmas light. The light was the truth of God's real presence with them . . . at that very moment . . . in their cell. Christ was there! He knew what they were experiencing. He understood, and He would help.

"*Immanuel*"

This Christmas season, write yourself a card with the word "*Immanuel*" on it.

When you get up in the morning, read it: *Immanuel!*

When you face trouble of any kind, read it: *Immanuel!*

When you walk alone, when you talk on the phone, when you meet a friend, when you go to work or church or home, read your reminder: *Immanuel!*

The truth of that name will keep you steady and strong and happy, not just at Christmas, but throughout the coming year. God is with you, and "*in His presence is fullness of joy*"!

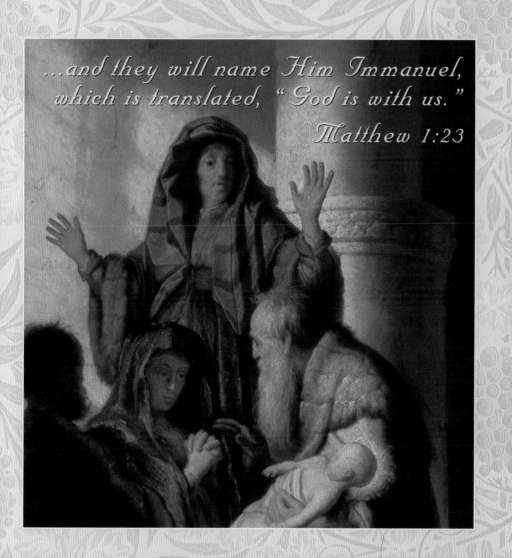

...and they will name Him Immanuel, which is translated, "God is with us."

Matthew 1:23

Celebrate with us
"Immanuel"—

God in Christ come down on earth to dwell.

Hold within your heart

His awesome nearness;

Celebrate the Holy Presence' dearness.

Christmas joy for us can last all year:

He is here, good friend!

He's really here!

Have you ever been where God is not?

"GOD with us." What a great name—an accurate name—for the Lord Jesus: "GOD."

This truth of God's being with us wasn't new that first Christmas; God had been with people in the past. He'd told Israel, for instance, that in the tabernacle or temple He would meet with them.

But when Jesus came, God reversed it from "Come meet Me in a certain place" to "I am now come to meet you. I've made the first move. I am 'Immanuel.'"

He went from eternity to time. He went from all of heaven to earth, to be literally "with us." Jesus is God, come to join us; He is God settled down among us.

The Gospel of Matthew begins with it: *"They will name Him Immanuel . . . 'God is with us.'"* And later, Matthew ends with Jesus' saying, *"And remember, I am with you always, to the end of the age."*

You cannot be where God is not.

"With" in the King James Version of the Bible is not only a preposition; it's also a noun. In Judges 16:7, Samson declared that his strength would leave him if he were tied with seven "withs." It was a word for vines so fresh and strong that they were virtually impossible to break. When two things were tied with "withs," they were together for good!

> *"And 'round my heart still closely twined*
> *Those cords which naught can sever,*
> *For I am His and He is mine*
> *Forever and forever!"*

Friend, think about it; hug it to your heart:

In times of threatened health, *Immanuel!*

In times of financial crunch, *Immanuel!*

In times of spiritual doubt, *Immanuel!*

In times of job problems, *Immanuel!*

In times of bereavement, *Immanuel!*

In times of difficulties, *Immanuel!*

As you right now think on this, *Immanuel!*

Through all your Christmas season and beyond, *Immanuel!*

You're safe.
God is with you.

He has been with you.
He is with you now.
And He will be with you…
Always.

Why settle for "God with me" when you can have "God with us"?

Jesus moved steadily, determinedly, from heaven to the manger, to the cross, to the resurrection, and then to His Church — His own ones. We're an occupied people! And we take our place as His people with all who have loved and followed Him for two thousand years — as well as with all those who follow Him today.

He is God with us, together. We are at our best when we treat each other with care and love, because Christ is with each one of us, and yet also, with all of us. He is Immanuel!

Moses insisted on the literal presence of the Lord as he led God's people forward together toward the Promised Land. He said, *"If your Presence does not go with us, do not send us up from here. How will anyone know that you are pleased with me and with your people unless* you go with us? What else will distinguish me and your people from all the other people on the face of the earth?" (Exodus 33:15–16, NIV).

And the God of grace and glory said to Moses, *"My Presence will go with you, and I will give you rest"* (Exodus 33:14, NIV).

Oh, insist on the presence of Immanuel for your whole family, for your whole church! If the circle is incomplete right now, or at odds with each other, intercede for them passionately, as Moses did! Ask the Lord, *"How will anyone know that You are pleased with me, with us —?"* Ask Him, *"What else will distinguish us from all the other people of the earth —?"*

Lead the way in apologies to your family, your church; be humble; be broken; take the low road. And behind the scenes . . . pray and pray and pray.

"Immanuel" means "God with us —together!"

"The LORD is in His Holy House."
Oh, grace beyond describing,
That Christ should please to dwell in me,
Immanuel residing!
"My soul doth magnify the Lord,"
I sing with little Mary,
That God should choose to enter in
This humble sanctuary!

Not now in little Bethlehem,
As in the tender story;
Not now upon the mercy seat,
The bright Shekinah glory,
But in the body of His saint
He now makes His residing—
Both He in me and I in Him,
In fellowship abiding.

Within my heart, a burning bush;
Within, a mountain smoking;
This flesh of mine, a temple veil,
The wondrous Presence cloaking;
Within this broken earthenware
A high and holy treasure:
Oh, mystery of mysteries!
Oh, grace beyond all measure!

"The LORD is in His Holy House."
Mysterious habitation!
I feel His Presence here within
And offer my oblation.
Keep burning, incense of my soul!
Keep cleansing me, O laver!
I want to serve and praise my God
Forever and forever!

Family Reflections

Last July the family was at daughter Margie and John's house, celebrating Ray's birthday. (Ray says, "Patriarch, with the accent on the first syllable—pay!")

What a mob! Daughter Sherry and Walt were there with two of their three: Mindy, youth worker on the staff of their church, and Beth Anne at Biola University. Drew was ministering in Mongolia with other teenagers for the summer.

Margie and John's offspring were there: Lisa and husband Mark with their toddlers, William and Wesley; Laurie and husband Mike with their little Kaitlin and Patrick; John IV and bride Becky.

Ray, Jr., had flown in for the party from Augusta, leaving behind wife Jani, as well as children Eric (student at Trinity Evangelical Divinity School), Krista and Dane (both at Wheaton College), and high schooler Gavin.

Nels and Heather were there with little sons Bradford and Robbie.

We ate a glorious meal with the volume level at the ceiling. Eventually the two little grandsons and the four great grandchildren disappeared off to bed. Whew!

The remaining seventeen of us gathered in the living room to talk, laugh, share silly cards, and eventually get down to our birthday party ritual: telling what we love about the birthday person and then having group prayer for that one.

It was a tender time—precious, as always. Our birthday parties are times to be guarded carefully (we're all busy people) and times to be cherished. God alone knows how long the circle will be unbroken.

Beautiful things were said to Ray, godly things with deep meanings.

Along the way, Mike (married to granddaughter Laurie) spoke. "I remember the first family birthday party I got invited to. Laurie and I were dating," he said. "Oh, my gosh! My eyes and ears couldn't get enough. So much love! Sins were prayed for, joys got expressed. It was a "God thing." I thought, *The Lord is here. The Lord is within this circle of people. This is awesome! I want into this family!*" (Laughter.)

Then he said very kind things about the Birthday Boy.

Ray ended the prayer time something like this:

"Father, who am I? Who are any of us? We are all at best unprofitable servants. We have nothing good in us, in ourselves. Lord—and that's all right.

"May our family only be explainable by the fact that you are our God! Individually and together, You have saved us, and You are with us! You are our Immanuel!

"Oh, as long as we live may we each choose only to walk with You, by You, for You, in You—obedient to You, drawing from You, dependent on You, loving You.

"Continue to be Immanuel to us, O Lord! As John and Charles Wesley said, *'And best of all, God is with us!'*"

Do not be afraid...

Said God to trembling Jacob, "Do not be afraid;
Go down to Egypt; I will bless you there."
Said God to threatened Israel, "Do not be afraid;
I'll guard you with my tender, loving care."

Said God through Christmas angels, "Do not be afraid;
Your Savior has been born; be full of cheer!
The price for all your trespasses will soon be paid.
Believe how much I love you! Do not fear."

And through the centuries since, and in the days ahead,
He is Almighty God! He'll lead as He has led.
His mercies will endure. His grace will aid.
So Merry Christmas! Do not be afraid.

List of Illustrations:

STATE REPORTS

The West

ARIZONA ★ NEVADA ★ UTAH

By

Thomas G. Aylesworth
Virginia L. Aylesworth

CHELSEA HOUSE PUBLISHERS
New York   Philadelphia

Produced by James Charlton Associates
New York, New York.

First Printing

1   3   5   7   9   8   6   4   2

Library of Congress Cataloging-in-Publication Data

Aylesworth, Thomas G.
    The West: Arizona, Nevada, Utah/by
Thomas G. Aylesworth and Virginia L. Aylesworth.
    p.   cm. — (State reports)
    Includes bibliographical references and index.
    Summary: Discusses geographical, historical, and cultural aspects
    of Arizona, Nevada, and Utah. Includes maps, illustrated fact
    spreads, and other relevant material.
    ISBN 0-7910-1049-X.
        0-7910-1396-0 (pbk.)
    1. West (U.S.)—Juvenile literature. 2. Arizona—Juvenile literature. 3. Nevada—Juvenile
literature. 4. Utah—Juvenile literature. [1. Arizona. 2. Nevada. 3. Utah. 4. West (U.S.)]
I. Aylesworth, Virginia L. II. Title. III. Series: Aylesworth, Thomas G. State reports.

F591.A95   1992   91-19394
979—dc20   CIP
                                                 AC

Contents

Arizona

The state seal of Arizona, adopted in 1910, is circular. In the center is a shield on which are pictured a miner standing in the mountains; fields; and a cow. These represent the state's minerals industry and agriculture. In the background are mountains, with the sun rising behind them. There is also a storage reservoir, a quartz mill, and a dam. Over all of this is the state motto, and around the edge is printed "Great Seal of the State of Arizona" and "1912," the year of the state's entry into the Union.

State Flag

The state flag was adopted in 1917. The lower half consists of a solid blue band. In the center is a copper-colored star, and radiating from the star upward are six yellow rays alternating with seven red rays. The star represents the state's chief mineral product, copper. The rays of the setting sun represent the state's location in the west.

State Motto

Ditat Deus

This Latin phrase means "God enriches," and it was selected in 1864.

The Grand Canyon, made a national park in 1919, attracts over 3 million visitors a year.

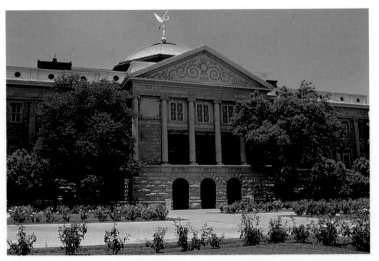

The old capitol is now the home of the Arizona State Capitol Museum.

State Capital

Phoenix has been the capital of Arizona since 1889, long before statehood. The capitol building was completed in 1900 at a cost of about $135,744. It is in the Victorian style and is constructed from Arizona materials—granite, tuff stone, and malapai.

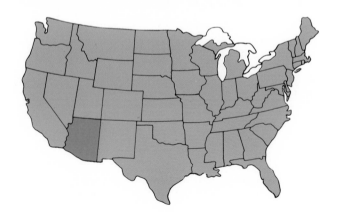

State Name and Nicknames

The Spanish gave Arizona its name in 1736. They took it from two words in the Papago Indian dialect, *Alehzon*, which means "little spring." Actually, the spring referred to is now in Mexico.

The most common nickname for Arizona is the *Grand Canyon State*. It is also known as the *Copper State* for its mining, and the *Apache State* for the Indians who once lived there.

State Flower

The bloom of the giant

The red bloom of the saguaro cactus is the state flower.

saguaro cactus, *Carnagiea gigantea*, has been the state flower since 1931.

State Tree

Adopted in 1954, the state tree of Arizona is the paloverde, *Cercidium torreyanum*.

State Bird

The cactus wren, *Heleodytes brunneicapillus*, was chosen the state bird in 1931.

State Gem

In 1974, turquoise was picked as the state gem.

State Neckwear

The bola tie was named the state neckwear in 1973.

State Song

The state song of Arizona is "Arizona March Song," with words by Margaret Rowe Clifford and music by Maurice Blumenthal.

Population

The population of Arizona in 1990 was 3,677,985, making

The cactus wren is the state bird.

it the 24th most populous state. There are 32.3 persons per square mile—83.8 percent of the population live in towns and cities. About 94 percent of the people in Arizona were born in the United States.

Geography and Climate

Bounded on the east by New Mexico, on the south by the Mexican state of Sonora, on the west by California, Nevada, and Mexico, and on the north by Utah, Arizona has an area of 114,000 square miles, making it the sixth largest state. The climate is clear and dry in the southern

A dramatic view of the Sonoran Desert.

manufactured products are electronics, printing and publishing, foods, primary and fabricated metals, aircraft and missiles, and apparel.

Agriculture

The chief crops of the state are cotton, sorghum, barley, corn, wheat, sugar beets, and citrus fruits. Arizona is also a livestock state, and there are estimated to be some 830,000 cattle, 100,000 hogs and pigs, 262,000 sheep, and 320,000 chickens on its farms. Pine, fir, and spruce trees are harvested. Copper,

Two participants in the Loggers' Festival at Payson, Arizona. Timber is one of the state's important agricultural products.

regions and northern plateaus, but there are heavy winter snows in the high central areas.

Highlands run from the northwest to the southeast. In the southwest is the Sonoran Desert. The highest point in the state, at 12,633 feet, is atop Humphreys Peak in Coconino County. The lowest, at 70 feet, is along the Colorado River in Yuma County. The major

waterways in the state are the Colorado, Bill Williams, Little Colorado, San Pedro, and Santa Cruz rivers. The largest lakes in the state, Theodore Roosevelt Lake and San Carlos Reservoir, are man-made.

Industries

The principal industries of Arizona are tourism, manufacturing, mining, and agriculture. The chief

These and other petroglyphs illustrate the lives and cultures of ancient indian civilizations.

molybdenum, gold, and silver are important mineral resources.

Government

The governor of Arizona is elected to a four-year term, as are the secretary of state, attorney general, state treasurer, and superintendent of public instruction. The state legislature, which meets annually, consists of a 30-member senate and a 60-member house of representatives. All the members serve two-year terms. Each of the 30 legislative districts elects one senator and two representatives for two-year terms. The most recent state constitution was adopted in 1910. In addition to its two U.S. senators, Arizona has six representatives in the House of Representatives. The state has eight votes in the electoral college.

History

Before Europeans arrived in what was to become Arizona, the area was inhabited by Anasazi, Hohokam, and Mogollon Indians. The Anasazi, who lived in the north, were the ancestors of the present-day Pueblo Indians. The Hohokam, who lived in the Gila River Valley, were the precursors of the Papago and Pima Indians. The Mogollon lived in eastern Arizona. Just before the coming of the Europeans, Apache and Navajo moved into the area.

Marcos de Niza, a Spanish Franciscan priest, entered the territory in 1539 during his search for the Seven Cities. In 1540, the Spanish explorer Francisco Vásquez de Coronado arrived, searching for gold. In the 1600s, the Roman Catholic Church began sending missionaries to Arizona, and in 1692,

Father Eusebio Francisco Kino began establishing missions in the territory. He was to found 24 of these. The Indians tried several times to drive out the Spanish but were unsuccessful. The first Spanish settlement, a fort at Tubac, was founded in 1752. Tucson became a Spanish fort in 1776.

Mexico gained its freedom from Spain in 1821, and the Mexican flag flew over Arizona. Arizona became part of the United States in 1848, after the Mexican War. The present boundary between the U.S. and Mexico was established as a result of the 1853 Gadsden Purchase, which added the land south of the Gila River to Arizona. During the Civil War, the Confederacy occupied the region, but was defeated by Union troops. In 1863, the Arizona Territory was created. Fighting Indians was one of the chief concerns of the Arizona settlers until 1886.

Despite the Indian wars, Arizona prospered. Gold and silver were mined, and irrigation was begun in 1867. Copper mining developed in the 1870s and 1880s, and the railroad arrived in 1877. Arizona became the 48th state of the Union in 1912.

Mining and agriculture continued to grow, and many dams were built to provide irrigation water. During World War II, the state was the home of several new air bases, and the demand for Arizona cattle, copper, and cotton rose. Today, the population is growing, and tourists are flocking to the state. Arizona is a land of contrasts—modern and prehistoric civilizations, mountains and deserts, arid wasteland and modern agriculture.

Although it is unclear why the right tower of the San Xavier del Bac Mission was never finished, it remains one of the best examples of Spanish Baroque architecture in the southwest.

Football fans in Arizona have the choice of cheering either the college team of Arizona State University or of the University of Arizona, or the NFL Phoenix Cardinals.

Sports

Arizona is a sports state and a real hotbed of collegiate baseball. The NCAA championship in that sport has been won by Arizona State University (1965, 1967, 1969, 1977, 1981) and the University of Arizona (1976, 1980, 1986). In football, Arizona State won the Rose Bowl in 1987.

On the professional level, the Phoenix Suns of the National Basketball

Association play in the Arizona Veterans' Memorial Coliseum, and the Phoenix Cardinals of the National Football League play in Sun Devil Stadium in Tempe.

Major Cities

Mesa (population 152,453). Founded in 1878, it was named Mesa—Spanish for "tabletop"—because it lies atop a plateau. The town is one of Arizona's fastest-growing communities.

Things to see in Mesa: Mormon Temple Visitors' Center, Mesa Southwest Museum, Arizona Museum for Youth, Champlin Fighter Museum, Rockin' R Ranch, and Lost Dutchman State Park.

Phoenix (population 789,704). Settled in 1864, the capital city has a glorious climate that attracts many tourists and retirees. It is surrounded by mountains and green irrigated fields.

Things to see in Phoenix: Arizona State Capitol Museum, Arizona Museum, Heard Museum of Anthropology and Primitive Art, Arizona Hall of Fame Museum, Desert

The variety and beauty of desert flora is displayed at the Desert Botanical Garden in Phoenix, Arizona.

Old Tucson was built in 1939 as the set for the movie Arizona at a cost of $250,000.

The Mystery Castle, built by Boyce Luther Gulley as a "live-in sandcastle" for his daughter, is made of native stone and is located near Phoenix.

Botanical Garden, Phoenix Zoo, Hall of Flame, Pueblo Grande Museum, Phoenix Art Museum, Arizona Mineral Museum, Encanto Park, Arizona History Room, Arizona Historical Society Museum, Arizona Museum of Science and Technology, Bayless Country Store Museum, Heritage Square, Mystery Castle, and Phoenix Mountain Preserve.

Tucson (population 330,537). Founded in 1775, Tucson has existed under four flags: Spain, Mexico, the Confederate States of America, and the United States of America. Today it is a center for health care, tourism, education, mining, and aircraft production.

Things to see in Tucson: Mission San Xavier del Bac, Arizona State Museum, Museum of Art and Faculty of Fine Arts, Mineralogical Museum, Grace H. Flandrau Planetarium, Center for Creative Photography, Arizona Historical Society Museum, Arizona Historical Society Frémont House Museum, Tucson Museum of Art, Arizona Historical Society Fort Lowell Museum, Pima Air Museum, Old Town

Artisans, Tucson Botanical Gardens, Old Pueblo Museum, International Wildlife Museum, Tohono Chul Park, Arizona-Sonora Desert Museum, Old Tucson, and Colossal Cave.

Places to Visit

The National Park Service maintains 28 areas in the state of Arizona: Grand Canyon National Park, Petrified Forest National Park, Canyon de Chelly National Monument, Casa Grande National Monument, Chiricahua National Monument, Montezuma Castle National Monument, Navajo National Monument, Organ Pipe Cactus National Monument, Pipe Spring National Monument, Saguaro National Monument, Sunset Crater National Monument, Tumacacori National Monument, Wupatki National Monument, Tonto National Monument, Tuzigoot National Monument, Walnut Canyon National Monument, Hohokam Pima National

Visitors touring the Queen Mine in Bisbee. Copper was first discovered there in 1875 by a prospector who was actually looking for silver or gold.

Monument, Coronado National Memorial, Glen Canyon Recreation Area, Lake Mead National Recreation Area, Hubbell Trading Post Historic Site, Fort Bowie National Historic Site, Apache-Sitgreaves National Forest, Coconino National Forest, Coronado National Memorial Forest, Kaibab Indian Preservation, Prescott National Forest, and Tonto National Monument.

In addition, there are 12 state recreation areas.

Bisbee: Queen Mine Tour. Visitors may take a one-and-a-half-hour guided tour on a copper mine train.

Camp Verde: Fort Verde State Historical Park. Four original buildings remain of this Indian Wars fort.

Chandler: Gila Bend Indian Reservation. More than 30 Indian tribes are represented in this artist and artisan center.

Flagstaff: Lowell Observatory. It was from here that the planet

Pluto was discovered in 1930.
Gila Bend: Painted Rocks State Park. Ancient Indian rock paintings can be seen here.
Globe: Besh-Ba-Gowah Indian Ruins. These ruins of a Salado Indian village date back more

than 700 years.
Jerome: This is an old copper-mining town with cobblestone streets.
Kingman: Bonelli House. Built in 1894, this building has been restored and contains many

original pieces.
Lake Havasu City: London Bridge English Village. This 21-acre village features the original London Bridge.
Litchfield Park: Wildlife World Zoo. The zoo houses exotic

London Bridge, built in 1831, was purchased by Robert McCulloch and relocated to Lake Havasu City in 1971. It connects an island in the lake with the mainland.

animals and a children's petting zoo.

Nogales: Tubac Presidio State Historical Park. The ruins of Arizona's first European settlement, built in 1752, can be seen here.

Patagonia: Stradling Museum of the Horse. Exhibits tell the story of the horse from ancient Greek times.

Prescott: Sharlot Hall Museum. This contains the old governor's mansion (1864) and other structures.

Scottsdale: Taliesin West. This is the winter campus of the Frank Lloyd Wright Foundation.

Sedona: Tlaquepaque. Art galleries and stores are located in a Spanish-style courtyard.

Sierra Vista: Fort Huachuca. The "old post" area dates back to 1885.

Superior: Boyce Thompson Southwestern Arboretum. Semi-desert plants from around the world can be seen on this 420-acre tract.

Tempe: Niels Petersen House. This Victorian home was built in 1892.

Tombstone: Bird Cage Theatre. This frontier cabaret was built in the 1880s.

Wickenburg: Frontier Street. The street has been preserved as it was in the early 1900s.

Sharlot Hall Museum in Prescott, Arizona, served as the territorial capitol from 1863 to 1867, and from 1877 to 1889.

The Tlaquepaque courtyard is home to a number of galleries and boutiques.

Window Rock: Navajo Tribal Museum. Exhibits show Navajo history, art, and culture.

Winslow: Meteor Crater. The world's best-preserved meteorite crater measures 4,150 feet from rim to rim.

Yuma: Yuma Territorial Prison State Historic Park. The ruins of the 1876 prison can be seen here.

Events

There are many events and organizations that schedule activities of various kinds in the state of Arizona. Here are some of them:

Sports: La Vuelta de Bisbee (Bisbee), Fiesta Days (Carefree), Horse races (Douglas), Cochise County Fair and College Rodeo (Douglas), Junior Parade (Florence), Thunderbird Balloon Classic 100 Hot-Air Balloon Race and Air Show (Glendale), Copper Dust Stampede Days (Globe), Navajo County Horse Races (Greer), Chili Cook-Off (Kingman), Havasu Classic Outboard World Championships (Lake Havasu City), Parker-Score 400 Off Road Race (Parker), Enduro Boat Race (Parker), All-Indian Rodeo (Parker), Sawdust Festival, Loggers' Competition (Payson), World's Oldest Continuous PRCA Rodeo (Payson), Aid to Zoo National Horse Show (Phoenix), LPGA Samaritan Turquoise Classic (Phoenix), National Hot Rod Association Drag Racing (Phoenix), Phoenix Formula I Grand Prix (Phoenix), World's Championship Jaycees Rodeo of Rodeos (Phoenix), Prescott Frontier Days Rodeo (Prescott), Parada del Sol and Rodeo (Scottsdale), Rodeo (Show Low), Fiesta Bowl Football Classic (Tempe), La Fiesta de los Vaqueros Rodeo (Tucson), Tucson Balloon Festival (Tucson), Tucson Open (Tucson), Rex Allen Days PRCA Rodeo (Willcox), Bill Williams Rendezvous Days (Williams), Cowpunchers' Reunion and Old-Timers' Rodeo (Williams), Powwow and PRCA Rodeo (Window Rock), Thoroughbred and Quarter Horse Racing (Yuma).

Arts and Crafts: Hopi Artists' Exhibition (Flagstaff), Navajo Artists' Exhibition (Flagstaff), Annual Vahki Exhibition (Mesa), Cactus Show (Phoenix), Cowboy Artists of America Exhibition (Phoenix), Gem and Mineral

The A to Z Horse Show is held every January to benefit the Phoenix Zoo.

Cowboys making their grand entrance to the rodeo. The first formal rodeo was held at Prescott, Arizona, in 1888.

Show (Phoenix), George Phippen Memorial Western Art Show (Prescott), Territorial Prescott Days (Prescott), Art in the Park (Sierra Vista), Winter Arts Festival (Sierra Vista), Festival of the Arts (Tubac), Gem and Mineral Show (Tucson), Southwest Antique Guild Show and Sale (Yuma).

Music: Country Music Festival (Flagstaff), Flagstaff Festival of the Arts (Flagstaff), Old-Time Fiddlers Contest (Globe), Square Dance Festival (Globe), Country Music Festival (Payson), Old-Time Fiddlers Contest and Festival (Payson), Arizona Opera Company (Phoenix), Ballet Arizona (Phoenix), Phoenix

Symphony (Phoenix), Phoenix Chamber Music Society (Phoenix), Arizona State University Lyric Opera (Phoenix), Phoenix Boys Choir (Phoenix), Valley of the Sun Annual Square and Round Dance Festival (Phoenix), Bluegrass Festival (Prescott), Southern Arizona Light Opera

The boats are the floats in the Lighted Boat Parade held in Parker, Arizona.

Company (Tucson), Tucson Pops Orchestra (Tucson), Arizona Opera Company (Tucson), Southern Arizona Square and Round Dance Festival (Tucson), Tucson Symphony (Tucson), Four Corners States Bluegrass Music Finals (Wickenburg).

Entertainment: Lost Dutchman Days (Apache Junction), Billy Moore Days (Avondale), O'Odham Tash-Casa Grande's Indian Days (Casa Grande), Verde Valley Fair (Cottonwood), Fort Verde Days (Cottonwood), Cinco de Mayo (Douglas), Fiesta Patrias (Douglas), Coconino County Fair (Flagstaff), Gila County Fair (Globe), Billy Moore Days (Goodyear), Navajo County Fair (Greer), Mohave

County Fair (Kingman), London Bridge Days (Lake Havasu City), Mesa Youthfest (Mesa), Cinco de Mayo Fiesta (Nogales), La Paz County Fair (Parker), Holiday Lighted Boat Parade (Parker), Fiesta Bowl Parade (Phoenix), Indian Fair (Phoenix), Maricopa County Fair (Phoenix), National Livestock Show (Phoenix), Yaqui Indian Holy Week Ceremonials (Phoenix), Agricultural Trade Fair (Phoenix), Arizona State Fair (Phoenix), Smoki Ceremonial and Snake Dance (Prescott), Yavapai County Fair (Prescott), Fiesta de Mayo (Safford), Pioneer Days (Safford), Graham County Fair (Safford), All-Arabian Horse Show (Scottsdale), Fiesta del Tlaquepaque (Sedona), Festival of Lights at Tlaquepaque (Sedona), Christmas Parade (Sierra Vista), Coronado Borderlands Festival (Sierra Vista), Springfest (Tempe), Fiesta Bowl Pep Rally (Tempe), Territorial Days (Tombstone), Wyatt Earp Days (Tombstone), Wild West Days and Rendezvous of Gunfighters (Tombstone), "Helldorado" (Tombstone), Oktoberfest (Tucson), Pima County Fair (Tucson), Pioneer Days at Fort Lowell Park (Tucson), Tucson Festival (Tucson), Fiesta del Presidio (Tucson), San Xavier Pageant and Fiesta (Tucson), Yaqui Indian Easter Ceremony (Tucson), Gold Rush Days (Wickenburg), Navajo Nation Fair (Window Rock), Yuma County Fair (Yuma).

Tours: Paseo de Casas (Cottonwood), Grand Canyon Helicopter Tours (Grand Canyon National Park), Yuma River Tours (Yuma).

Theater: Arizona Theatre Company (Phoenix), The Phoenix Little Theatre (Phoenix), Stagebrush Theater (Phoenix), Celebrity Theatre (Phoenix), Gaslight Theatre (Tucson), The Invisible Theatre (Tucson), Arizona Theatre Company (Tucson).

Famous People

Many famous people were born in the state of Arizona. Here are a few:

Rose Elizabeth Bird b. 1936, Tucson. Chief justice of the California supreme court

Cesar Chavez b. 1927, Yuma. Union leader

Cochise 1812-74, Apache leader

Joan Ganz Cooney b. 1929, Phoenix. Founder of Children's TV Workshop, producer of *Sesame Street*

John Denny b. 1952, Prescott. Baseball pitcher

Andy Devine 1905-77, Flagstaff. Cowboy film comedian

Barbara Eden b. 1934, Tucson. Television actress: *I Dream of Jeannie*

Sean Elliott b. 1968, Tucson. Basketball player

Gary Gentry b. 1946, Phoenix. Baseball pitcher

Geronimo 1829-1909, Apache leader

Geronimo was the leader of the Chiricahua Apaches, although he was not a Chiricahua by birth.

Morris K. Udall served Arizona as a member of the U.S. House of Representatives for 30 years.

Barry Goldwater b. 1909, Phoenix. Senate leader and presidential candidate
Billy Hatcher b. 1960, Williams. Baseball player
Carl Hayden 1877-1972, Tempe. Senate leader
Richard B. Kleindienst b. 1923, near Winslow.

U.S. attorney general
Charlie Mingus 1922-79, Nogales. Jazz bassist
Sandra Day O'Connor b. 1930, near Duncan. U.S. Supreme Court justice
Alexander M. Patch 1889-1945, Fort Huachuca, Arizona Territory. Army officer
Marty Robbins 1925-82, Glendale. Country-and-western singer
Linda Ronstadt b. 1946, Tucson. Pop singer
Paul Silas b. 1943, Prescott. Basketball player
Morris K. Udall b. 1922, St. Johns. Congressman
Stewart L. Udall b. 1920, St. Johns. U.S. secretary of the interior

Colleges and Universities
There are many colleges and universities in Arizona. Here are the more prominent, with

their locations, dates of founding, and enrollments.
Arizona State University, Tempe, 1885, 43,546
DeVry Institute of Technology, Phoenix, 1967, 2,699
Embry-Riddle Aeronautical University, Prescott, 1978, 1,771
Grand Canyon College , Phoenix, 1949, 1,842
Northern Arizona University, Flagstaff, 1899, 16,095
University of Arizona, Tucson, 1885, 35,569
University of Phoenix, Phoenix, 1976, 5,714
Western International University, Phoenix, 1978, 3,214

Where To Get More Information
Arizona Office of Tourism
1100 West Washington
Phoenix, AZ 85007
Or call 1-602-542-3618

Nevada

The state seal of Nevada, adopted in 1866, is circular. On it are depicted a plow and sheaf of wheat (representing agriculture) and a quartz mill, mine tunnel, and carload of ore (standing for mineral wealth). In the middle distance are a railroad train and telegraph lines. In the background, the sun rises behind a range of snow-capped mountains. Around the drawing are 36 stars (Nevada is the 36th state) and the state motto. Around the outside of the seal is printed "The Great Seal of the State of Nevada."

State Flag

The current state flag was adopted in 1929. It is blue, and in the upper corner nearest the staff is a silver star, under which are two crossed sprays of sagebrush. The letter *N* is located above the top point of the star, and the letters *E, V, A, D,* and *A* are located between the points. Above all this is the phrase "Battle Born," signifying the fact that Nevada was made a state during the Civil War.

State Motto

All For Our Country

This patriotic motto was selected in 1866.

The Snake Mountain Range in Nevada.

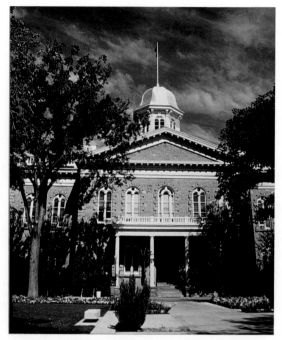

State Capital

Carson City has been the state capital since the creation of the Nevada Territory in 1861. The capitol building was completed in 1871 at a cost of $169,830. It is built of Nevada sandstone, and gigantic wooden beams support the roof.

Finished in 1871, the State Capitol was the work of Joseph Gosling, an architect from California. It has been likened to an "oversized courthouse."

State Name and Nicknames

The name Nevada was given to the region by seventeenth- and eighteenth-century Spanish sailors who were sailing between the Philippines and Mexico. They saw California mountain ranges from far out at sea and called them "Sierra Nevada," or "snowy range." When the Nevada Territory was created, it was first thought that it ought to be called Sierra Nevada, but this was quickly shortened to Nevada.

The mountain bluebird is the state bird.

The sagebrush, though it is unrelated to the herb sage, smells like sage.

Nevada has several nicknames. It is called the *Silver State* and the *Mining State* for its silver mines. It is also called the *Sage State* and the *Sagebrush State* for the wild sage that grows there, and the *Battle Born State* because it entered the Union during the Civil War.

State Flower

The sagebrush, *Artemisia tridentata*, was adopted as state flower in 1967. It had been the unofficial state blossom since 1917.

State Tree

Nevada has two official state trees. The single-leaf piñon, *Pinus monophylla*, was selected as state tree in 1959. In 1987, the bristlecone pine tree, *Pinus aristata*, was also designated state tree by the Nevada legislature.

The bristlecone pine is one of the two state trees.

State Bird

Adopted in 1967, the mountain bluebird, *Sialia currucoides*, is the state bird.

State Animal

The desert bighorn sheep, *Ovis canadensis*, has been the state animal since 1973.

State Rock

Sandstone is the official state rock.

State Colors

Silver and blue were named the colors of Nevada in 1983.

State Fish

The Lohonton cutthroat trout, *Salmo clarki*, was selected as state fish in 1981.

State Fossil

The state fossil, adopted in 1977, is the ichthyosaur, an extinct prehistoric marine reptile.

State Grass

Indian rice grass, *Oryzopsis hymenoides*, was named the state grass in 1977.

Bighorn, or Rocky Mountain sheep, are a favorite target of hunters, causing the animal's population to dwindle drastically.

State Metal

Silver was adopted as state metal in 1977.

State Song

In 1933, "Home Means Nevada," words and music by Bertha Raffetto, was named the state song of Nevada.

Population

The population of Nevada in 1990 was 1,206,152, making it the 39th most populous state. There are 10.9 persons per square mile—85.3 percent of the population live in towns and cities. About 93 percent of the people in Nevada were born in the United States.

Geography and Climate

Bounded on the east by Utah and Arizona, on the south by Arizona and California, on the west by

Lake Mead was created by the Hoover Dam and is the largest water project in the state.

California, and on the north by Oregon and Idaho, Nevada has an area of 110,561 square miles, making it the seventh largest state. The climate is semi-arid.

There are rugged mountains running from north to south, and in the south is desert land. The highest point in the state, at 13,140 feet, is atop Boundary Peak in Esmeralda County. The lowest, at 479 feet, is at Mount Manchester in Clark County. The major waterways of the state are the Virgin, Muddy, Colorado, Owyhee, Bruneau, Salmon, Humboldt, Carson, Walker, and Truckee rivers. Pyramid Lake is the largest natural lake within the borders of Nevada.

Industries

The principal industries of Nevada are gambling, gaming, tourism, mining, agriculture, manufacturing, government warehousing, and trucking. The chief manufactured products are gaming devices, chemicals, aerospace products, lawn and garden irrigation equipment, and seismic and machinery-monitoring devices.

Agriculture

The chief crops of the state are alfalfa seed, potatoes, hay, barley, and wheat. Nevada is also a livestock state. There are estimated to be some 500,000 cattle, 16,000 hogs and pigs, 96,000 sheep, and 18,000 chickens and turkeys on its farms. Piñon, juniper, and other pine trees are harvested. Gold, silver, barite, and construction sand and gravel are important mineral resources.

Government

The governor of Nevada is elected to a four-year term, as are the lieutenant governor, secretary of state, treasurer, controller, and attorney general. The state legislature, which meets in odd-numbered years, consists of a 21-member senate and a 42-member assembly. Senators, who serve four-year terms, are elected from Nevada's 21 senatorial districts. Assemblymen, who serve two-year terms, are elected from 42 assembly districts. Each senatorial and assembly district elects one member. The most recent state constitution was adopted in 1864. In addition to its two U.S. senators, Nevada has two representatives in the House of Representatives. The state has four votes in the electoral college.

History

Long before the Europeans arrived, what was to become Nevada was inhabited by cave-dwelling Indians. Basketmakers once lived at Lovelock Cave, and Pueblo Indians lived around what is now Las Vegas. When the European explorers first came, they found Mohave, Paiute, Shoshone, and

The Spring Mountains provide a backdrop for this alfalfa field near Pahrump.

Washoe Indians living in Nevada.

Perhaps the first European to enter the Nevada area was a Spanish missionary, Francisco Garcés, who may have passed through southern Nevada in 1776. But the first explorers were the fur traders and trappers who went there between 1825 and 1830. The Old Spanish Trail was blazed in 1830. It stretched from Santa Fe to Los Angeles, leaving Nevada open to trade from the southeast. Another trail across the Humboldt River was opened in 1833. Between 1843 and 1845, Lieutenant John C. Frémont explored the Great Basin and Sierra Nevada.

Nevada had been a part of Mexico until 1848, when, at the end of the Mexican War, it was turned over to the United States as a part of the large territory that also included California, Utah, and parts of four other states. In 1849, the Mormon leader Brigham Young organized Utah and most of present-day Nevada as the state of Deseret. Nevada then became part of the Utah Territory.

Mormons from the Great Salt Lake area began to settle the Carson Valley in Nevada in 1851, but Brigham Young called them back in 1857. In 1859, silver was discovered at the site of present-day Virginia City, and suddenly the town became a mining center. Because of the influx of people to Nevada, the Nevada Territory was created in 1861, and it became the 36th state of the Union in 1864.

The state was hurt by the drop in silver prices in the 1870s, but economic development was aided by the discovery of higher-grade silver at Tonopah in 1900 and the discovery of gold at Goldfield in 1902. Copper ore was also discovered at Ely,

Virginia City was founded in 1859, after gold was discovered on Mount Davidson. Silver was found a year later, speeding the growth of the boom town.

Hoover Dam, the largest dam ever built, manages to tame the mighty Colorado River, which carved out the Grand Canyon.

Ruth, and Mountain City. Railroads to the mining camps were opened, and these also gave the cattle ranchers a source of transportation for their animals.

During World War I, Nevada's copper, zinc, tungsten, and other metals became important to the war effort. In 1931, Nevada made gambling legal, and this industry came to provide large amounts of tax money for the state. The giant Hoover Dam (then called Boulder Dam) was completed in 1936 and began to supply huge amounts of electrical power and irrigation water. World War II created a new demand for the state's copper, lead, magnesite, manganese, tungsten, and zinc.

Today, Nevada is a tourist's mecca, as well as a land of history and tradition, magnificent scenery, and wild desert country.

Sports

Sports are popular in the state of Nevada. On the collegiate level, the NCAA basketball championship was won by the University of Nevada, Las Vegas, in 1990.

Major Cities

Carson City (population 32,022). Founded in 1858, the capital city is situated near the edge of the eastern slope of the Sierra Nevada. First called Eagle Ranch, it was renamed for the famous scout Kit Carson.

Things to see in Carson City: State Capitol, State Library

The lights of Las Vegas casinos.

Building, Nevada State Museum, Stewart Indian Museum, Warren Engine Company No. 1 Fire Museum, Nevada State Railroad Museum, and Bowers Mansion (1864).

Las Vegas (population 183,184). First settled in 1855 by Mormons, the town became a major entertainment center after World War II. It is a city of tree-lined avenues set in a desert environment.

Things to see in Las Vegas: The Strip, Convention Center, Liberace Museum, Las Vegas Art Museum, Las Vegas Museum of Natural History, Nevada State Museum and Historical Society, Donna Beam Fine Art Gallery, Old Mormon Fort, Ripley's "Believe It or Not," Imperial Palace Auto Collection, Wet 'n Wild, Spring Mountain Ranch, and Bonnie Springs Old Nevada.

Reno (population 100,756). Founded in 1868, the "Biggest

Little City in the World" was first known as Lake's Crossing. It was eventually renamed to honor General Jesse Lee Reno, a Union officer of the Civil War.

Things to see in Reno: Fleischmann Planetarium, Nevada Historical Society Museum, William F. Harrah Foundation National Automobile Museum, Wilbur D. May Museum and Arboretum, Mackay School of Mines Museum, and Sierra Nevada Museum of Art.

Places to Visit

The National Park Service maintains five areas in the state of Nevada: Lake Mead National Recreation Area, part of Death Valley National Monument, Great Basin National Park, Humboldt National Forest, and Toiyabe National Forest. In addition, there are 20 state recreation areas.

Austin: Stokes Castle. This three-story stone building can be seen for miles.

Elko: Northeastern Nevada Museum. Exhibits on the area's Indian heritage and mining tradition are featured.

The National Automobile Museum has displays illustrating every development of automotive history.

Ely: Nevada Northern Railway Museum. This museum is housed in the 1906 Nevada Northern Railway depot.

Fallon: Churchill County Museum and Archives. Memorabilia of the Pony Express and Transcontinental Telegraph are displayed.

Genoa: Mormon Station Historic Monument. This restored stockade and trading post was built in 1851.

Henderson: Ethel M. Chocolate Factory and Cactus Garden. Visitors may tour the factory and adjacent gardens, which contain 350 species of desert plants.

Incline Village: Ponderosa Ranch and Western Theme Park. Here is the Cartwright House of the *Bonanza* television series.

Lovelock: Courthouse Park. The only round courthouse still in use is located here.

Overton: Lost City Museum of Archeology. Several Pueblo-type houses and Indian relics dating back 10,000 years are featured.

Sparks: Wild Island. This amusement area contains water rides, a game arcade, and miniature golf.

Tonopah: Mizpah Hotel. Built in 1907, this restored mining hotel is a Victorian building.

Virginia City: The Castle. Built in 1868, this was styled after a castle in Normandy, France.

Winnemucca: Humboldt Museum. Exhibits here feature Indian and pioneer artifacts.

Yerington: Fort Churchill Historic State Monument. This post was garrisoned from 1860 to 1869 as a defense against the Paiute Indians.

Participants race for the finish line in the Bristlecone Chariot Races.

Events

There are many events and organizations that schedule activities of various kinds in the state of Nevada. Here are some of them:

Sports: Lincoln County Fair and Rodeo (Caliente), Whistle-Off (Carson City), Elko Expo Open (Elko), Western Festival (Elko), Bristlecone Birkebeiner Ski Race (Ely), Bristlecone Chariot Races (Ely), Wild Bunch Stampede Rodeo (Fallon), All Indian Rodeo (Fallon), US Bass Lake Mead National Draw Tournament (Lake Mead), Las Vegas Invitational Golf Tournament (Las Vegas), Imperial Palace Antique Auto Run (Las Vegas), Showboat Invitational Bowling Tournament (Las Vegas), World Series of Poker (Las Vegas), National Finals Rodeo (Las Vegas), Nissan/Mint 400 Off-Road Race (Las Vegas), Winter Carnival (Reno), Snafflebit Futurity (Reno), Great Balloon Race (Reno), Reno Rodeo (Reno), National Championship Air Races (Reno), National Championship Camel Races (Virginia City), 100-Mile Horse Endurance Race (Virginia City), Wells Pony Express Race (Wells), Tri-County Fair and Oldest Nevada Rodeo (Winnemucca).

More than 6,000 people convene every year to hear working cowboys recite traditonal and original cowboy poetry at the Cowboy Poetry Gathering in Elko.

White Pine County Fair (Ely), Carson Valley Days (Gardnerville), Industrial Days (Henderson), Lake Mead Parade of Lights (Lake Mead), All Indian Powwow (Las Vegas), Helldorado Festival (Las Vegas), Jaycee State Fair (Las Vegas), Jerry Lewis Telethon (Las Vegas), Laughlin River Days (Laughlin), Frontier Days (Lovelock), Heritage Days (Pioche), Sparks Festival Days (Sparks), Jim Butler Days (Tonopah), Red Mountain Powwow (Winnemucca).

Tours: Lincoln County Art Room (Caliente), Hidden Cave Tours (Fallon), Ichthyosaur Fossil Shelter (Gabbs), Piper's Opera House (Virginia City).

Theater: Judy Bayley Theatre (Las Vegas), Reed Whipple Cultural Center (Las Vegas), Charleston Heights Arts Center (Las Vegas), Church Fine Arts Theatre (Reno).

Arts and Crafts: Outdoor Art Festival (Boulder), Cowboy Poetry Gathering (Elko), Western Art Round-Up (Winnemucca).

Music: Artemus W. Ham Concert Hall (Las Vegas), International Jazz Festival (Reno), Nevada Opera (Reno).

Entertainment: Battle Mountain Annual Crab Feed and Dance (Battle Mountain), Boulder Damboree (Boulder),

Lincoln County Homecoming (Caliente), Meadow Valley Western Days (Caliente), Kit Carson Rendezvous/Wagon Train Days (Carson City), Spring Fun Fair (Carson City), Nevada Day Celebration (Carson City), Cowboy Poetry Gathering (Elko), National Basque Festival (Elko), Mardi Gras (Elko), County Fair and Livestock Show (Elko), Pony Express Days (Ely),

Famous People

Many famous people were born in the state of Nevada. Here are a few:

Eva B. Adams b. 1908, Wonder. Director of U.S. Mint

Henry Fountain Ashurst 1874-1962, Winnemucca. Senate leader

Paul Laxalt is one of Nevada's most prominent public officials, having served as governor of the state as well as a two-term United States senator.

Jack Kramer b. 1921, Las Vegas. Champion tennis player

Paul Laxalt b. 1922, Reno. Senate leader

Robert C. Lynch 1880-1931, Carson City. Surgeon

Anne H. Martin 1875-1951, Empire City. Suffragist, author, and social critic

Pat McCarran 1876-1954, near Reno. Senate leader

Max McGee b. 1932, Saxton City. Football player

Maurice E. McLoughlin 1890-1957, Carson City. Champion tennis player

Charles Michelson 1868-1948, Virginia City. Journalist and political publicist

Jim Nash b. 1945, Hawthorne. Baseball pitcher

Pat Nixon b. 1912, Ely. Former first lady

Mark L. Requa 1865-1937, Virginia City. Mining engineer and political leader

Sarah Winnemucca 1844-91, near Humboldt Lake. Indian scout and interpreter

Wovoka 1856-1932, near Walker Lake. Indian mystic and originator of Ghost Dance religion

Colleges and Universities

There are two universities in the state of Nevada. Here are the two, with their locations, dates of founding, and enrollments.

University of Nevada, Las Vegas, Las Vegas, 1957, 16,320

University of Nevada, Reno, Reno, 1874, 10,093

Where To Get More Information

Nevada Commission on Tourism
Capitol Complex
Carson City NV 89710
Or call 1-800-NEVADA8

Utah

The state seal of Utah, adopted in 1896, is circular. In the center is a shield with a beehive, representing industry. To the left and right of the beehive are sego lilies, standing for peace. Below the beehive is the date 1847, the year the Mormons came to the Salt Lake Valley. The top of the shield is pierced by six arrows, under which is the word *Industry* on a banner. Over the shield is an American eagle with outstretched wings, and to each side of the shield is an American flag. Around the seal is printed "The Great Seal of the State of Utah" and "1896," the year Utah became a state.

State Flag

The state flag of Utah was adopted in 1913. On a blue field is the shield, eagle, and American flags from the state seal. Below the shield are the dates 1847 and 1896. A narrow gold circle surrounds the seal.

State Motto

Industry

The motto was adopted in 1896.

Colorful hot air balloons cross the Utah sky.

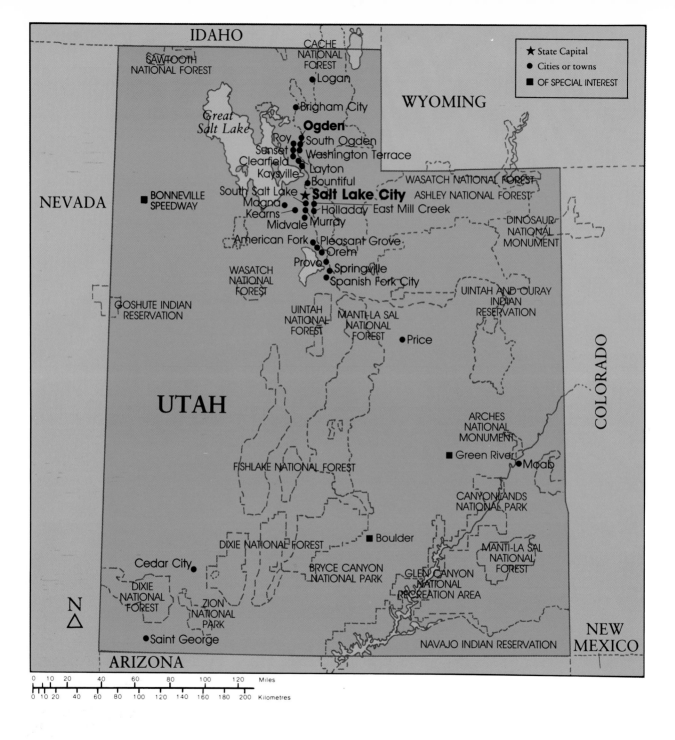

The architecture of the Utah State Capitol is based on the U.S. Capitol.

State Capital

  Salt Lake City has been the capital since 1856, forty years before Utah became a state. The capitol building was completed in 1915, at a cost of $2,739,528, and was built of Utah granite and Georgia marble in the Renaissance revival style. The dome, reaching a height of 165 feet, is supported by 24 Corinthian columns.

State Name and Nicknames

The White Mountain Apache Indians called the Navajo *Yuttahih,* which meant "one that is higher up." But early explorers thought that the word referred to the Ute, who lived higher in the mountains, so the land of the Utes became Utah.

The most common nickname for Utah is the *Beehive State,* the symbol of industry on the state seal and flag. Because it was settled by the Mormons, it is also called the *Mormon State* and the *Land of the Saints* (the Mormon church is officially called The Church of Jesus Christ of the Latter-Day Saints). Because of the Great Salt Lake, it is also referred to as the *Salt Lake State.*

State Flower

The sego lily, *Calochortus nuttalli,* was named the state flower of Utah in 1911.

State Tree

The blue spruce, *Picea pungens,* was selected as state tree in 1933.

These yellow blooms are the state flower of Utah.

State Bird

In 1955, the legislature adopted the California gull, *Larus californicus,* as state bird.

State Animal

The elk, *Cervus canadensis,* has been the state animal since 1971.

State Emblem

The beehive was named state emblem in 1959.

State Fish

The rainbow trout, *Salmo irideus,* was selected as the state fish in 1971.

State Gem

The topaz has been the state gem since 1969.

State Insect

The honeybee, *Apis mellifera,* was selected as state insect in 1983.

State Song

In 1937, "Utah We Love Thee," written by Evan Stephens, was adopted as the state song.

Population

The population of Utah in 1990 was 1,727,784, making it the 35th most populous state.

The seagull is the state bird of Utah.

There are 20.4 persons per square mile—84.4 percent of the population live in towns and cities. More than 95 percent of the people in Utah were born in the United States.

Geography and Climate

Bounded on the east by Wyoming and Colorado, on the south by Arizona, on the west by Nevada, and on the north by Idaho and Wyoming, Utah has an area of 84,899 square miles, making it the 11th largest state. The climate is arid, ranging from warm desert in the southwest to alpine in the northeast.

In the southeast is the high Colorado plateau, and in the west is the desertlike Great Basin. In the northwest are salt flats, and in the northeast are the Rocky Mountains. The highest point in the state, at 13,528 feet, is atop Kings Peak in Duchesne County. The lowest, at 2,000 feet, is along Beaverdam Wash in Washington County. The

Rocket boosters under construction at the Morton Thiokol plant.

major waterways in Utah are the Colorado, Green, Bear, Provo, Weber, and Sevier rivers. The Great Salt Lake is the largest lake west of the Mississippi River.

Industries

The principal industries of Utah are services, trade, manufacturing, government, and construction. The chief manufactured products are guided missiles and parts, electronic components, food products, fabricated metals, steel, and electrical equipment.

Agriculture

The chief crops of the state are wheat, hay, apples, barley, alfalfa seed, corn, potatoes, cherries, and onions. Utah is also a livestock state. There are estimated to be some 855,000 cattle, 34,000 hogs and pigs,

600,000 sheep, and 3.8 million chickens and turkeys on its farms. Aspen, spruce, and pine trees are harvested. Copper, gold, and magnesium are important mineral resources.

Government

The governor of Utah is elected to a four-year term, as are the attorney general, lieutenant governor, state auditor, and state treasurer.

The state legislature, which meets annually, consists of a 29-member senate and a 75-member house of representatives. Senators serve four-year terms and representatives serve two-year terms. They are elected from districts drawn up according to population. The most recent state constitution was adopted in 1895. In addition to its two U.S. senators, Utah has three

representatives in the House of Representatives. The state has five votes in the electoral college.

History

Before the Europeans arrived in what was to become Utah, the area was inhabited by cave- and pueblo-dwelling Indians. By 1776, there were four major tribes in the territory—the Gosiute, Paiute, Shoshone, and Ute. The Navajo, who now occupy large areas in the southwestern part of the state, did not arrive there until the 1860s.

Spanish explorers might have wandered into the area in 1540, but no one is sure. In 1776, however, two Spanish Franciscan friars, Silvestre Velez de Escalonte and Francisco Alamasio Domínguez, and their men explored the region and discovered Utah Lake, southeast of the Great Salt Lake. Later, other Spaniards ventured into Utah, but the Spanish government was not

A farm in Ogden Valley. Ogden served as the junction for transfers between the Union Pacific and the Central Pacific.

interested in founding any settlements there. In 1811-12, American fur traders came into northern Utah.

Jim Bridger, the famous scout, discovered the Great Salt Lake during the winter of 1824-25, although, because of the saltiness of the lake's water, he thought he had discovered an ocean. Hundreds of fur trappers and traders came to the Great Salt Lake area, and by 1830, many pioneers were passing through the area on the way from Santa Fe to Los Angeles.

It was the Mormons—members of the Church of Jesus Christ of Latter-Day Saints—who settled Utah. They had been victims of religious persecution almost everywhere they went. They traveled from New York to Ohio, Missouri, and Illinois, looking for religious freedom. The Mormon leader Brigham Young led a group of his people west in 1846. They reached the Great Salt Lake region—then considered a part of Mexico—the next year

The Mormon Tabernacle in Salt Lake City is famous for its fine acoustics.

and settled there. Over the next 40 years, many more Mormons arrived, and settlements were founded in many parts of the territory. In 1847, the United States defeated Mexico in the Mexican War, and by a treaty signed February 2, 1848, Utah was ceded to the United States.

The settlers had trouble with the Indians from time to time, beginning in 1853 and not ending until 1867. In 1849, the Mormons established the state of Deseret and asked to be admitted to the Union. In 1850, the Utah Territory was established, extending far to the east and west of present-day Utah. Between 1849 and 1895, Utah asked to enter the Union several times, but Congress balked because of the Mormon practice of polygamy. From 1858 to 1861,

The Kennecott copper mine is one of many in Utah.

Utah was governed by federal troops. When the Civil War broke out, these troops were withdrawn in order to fight in the war.

In the 1860s, the Utah boundaries were changed several times. Parts of the area were given to Nevada, Colorado, and Wyoming. In 1862, Congress passed a law against polygamy, and federal troops were again sent to Utah. In 1869, the Union Pacific and the Central Pacific railroads from the west met at Promontory, Utah, and the United States had a transcontinental railroad system. In 1895, Utah wrote a new constitution that outlawed polygamy, and became the 45th state in the Union in 1896.

The railroads expanded in the early 1900s, opening new markets for Utah's farming and mining products. Copper mining boomed, as did livestock raising. During World War I, the state supplied the war effort with large amounts of necessary metals. Utah suffered during the Great Depression of the 1930s, but industries prospered again during World War II as the state became one of the leading producers of copper, gold, lead, silver, and zinc.

After the war, industrial growth continued as the steel and oil industries prospered. Uranium was discovered in Utah, and the state became a missile-producing center for the United States government. Today, Utah is a leader in agriculture and industry. It is also a state of magnificent beauty, with mountains, lakes, forests, and living deserts.

Sports

Sports are popular in Utah. On the collegiate level, the NCAA basketball championship was won by the University of Utah in

1944. The National Invitation Tournament was won by the University of Utah (1947) and Brigham Young University (1951, 1966). On the professional level, the Utah Jazz of the National Basketball Association play in the Salt Palace in Salt Lake City.

Major Cities

Ogden (population 64,407). Settled in 1844, Ogden was laid out by Brigham Young in a geometrical style. Today it is a commercial and industrial center.

Things to see in Ogden:
Daughters of Utah Pioneers Visitors Center and Relic Hall, Union Station, Browning-Kimball Car Museum, Browning Firearms Museum, Pine View Reservoir, and Fort Buenaventura State Park.

Provo (population 73,108). Settled in 1849, this city, surrounded by high mountains, is an education and commercial center. It was named after the French-Canadian explorer Etienne

Karl "the Mailman" Malone, of the Utah Jazz. The team relocated from New Orleans in 1979 and has yet to change its nickname.

Temple Square, the center of the Mormon religion, lies within ten walled acres of Salt Lake City.

The Lion House was built in 1856 as a home for part of Brigham Young's large family.

Provost, who explored the area in 1825.

> *Things to see in Provo:* Secured Art Gallery, Harris Fine Arts Center, Eyring Science Center, Monte L. Bean Life Science Museum, Museum of Peoples and Cultures, McCurdy Historical Doll Museum, Pioneer Museum, Camp Floyd State Park, and Bridal Veil Falls Tramway.

Salt Lake City (population 163,697). Founded in 1847, the capital city, once the site of a desert wilderness, is a monument to the invincibility of the human spirit. It was laid out in a grid pattern and today is an industrious, businesslike city.

> *Things to see in Salt Lake City:* Temple Square, Tabernacle (1867), Temple (1893, closed to non-Mormons), Assembly Hall (1882), Seagull Monument (1913), Museum of Church History and Art, Family History Library, Salt Palace, Arrow Press Square, Brigham Young Monument, Lion House (1856), Beehive House (1854), State Capitol (1914), Council Hall, Governor's Mansion, Pioneer Memorial Museum, Carriage House, Hansen Planetarium

(1905), ZCMI (Zion's Co-operative Mercantile Institution), Salt Lake Art Center, Utah Museum of Fine Arts, Utah Museum of Natural History, State Arboretum, Trolley Square, Liberty Park, Raging Waters, "This Is the Place" Monument, Old Deseret Pioneer Village, Hogle Zoological Garden, 49th Street Galleria, Fort Douglas Military Museum, and Wheeler Historic Farm.

Places to Visit

The National Park Service maintains 21 areas in the state of Utah: Arches National Park, Bryce Canyon National Park, Canyonlands National Park, Capitol Reef National Park, Zion National Park, Cedar Breaks National Monument, Dinosaur National Monument, Natural Bridges National Monument, Rainbow Bridge National Monument, Timpanogos Cave National Monument, Hovenweep National

Capitol Reef National Park consists of eroded rocks of unusual shapes and colors.

Monument, Golden Spike National Historic Site, High Uintahs Wilderness Area, most of Glen Canyon National Recreation Area, most of Flaming Gorge Dam and National Recreation Area, Ashley National Forest, Dixie National Forest, Fishlake National Forest, Manti-LaSal National Forest, Uintah National Forest, and Wasatch-Cache National Forest. In addition, there are 29 state recreation areas.

Boulder: Anasazi Indian Village State Park. Visitors may tour the site where 87 rooms dating from A.D. 1050 have been excavated.

Brigham City: Brigham City Mormon Tabernacle. Built in 1881, this house of worship is still in use.

Cedar City: Iron Mission State Park. An extensive collection of pioneer horse-drawn vehicles and wagons is on display here, the site of the first iron foundry west of the Mississippi.

Farmington: Lagoon Amusement Park. This park features a replica of a 19th-century frontier settlement, stagecoach rides, and wild West entertainment.

Fillmore: Territorial Statehouse State Park. Utah's first territorial capitol is now a museum.

Green River: Goblin Valley State Park. This mile-wide basin is filled with oddly-eroded sandstone formations.

Heber City: Heber Creeper. Visitors may take a train ride through Heber Valley and Provo Canyon.

Kanab: Movie sets. Several movie locations can be seen in the area, including a false-front Western town.

Lehi: John Hutching's Museum of Natural History. The museum contains pioneer and Indian artifacts, fossils, a large mineral collection, and shell and bird specimens.

Logan: Ronald V. Jensen Historical Farm and Man and His Bread Museum. This re-creation of a typical pioneer farm includes exhibits on agricultural development

Goblin Valley is preserved as a Utah state park.

from the mid-1800s to the present.

Moab: Hollywood Stuntmen's Hall of Fame. Exhibits include stuntmen's costumes, weapons, photographs, and videos.

Park City: Egyptian Theatre.

Built in 1926, it was originally a silent-film theater and vaudeville house.

Price: College of Eastern Utah Prehistoric Museum. Displays of dinosaur remains and geological specimens are featured.

St. George: Brigham Young Winter Home. Built in 1873, this adobe home was used by Young during his last nine winters.

Springville: Springville Museum of Art. Exhibits feature works by Utah artists.

Vacationers hit the slopes of one of Utah's many fine ski resorts.

A snow sculpture rises majestically from the icy Utah winterscape.

Vernal: Utah Field House of Natural History. The gardens are designed to appear as they did during the age of the dinosaurs and contain 14 life-size dinosaur figures.

Events

There are many events and organizations that schedule activities of various kinds in the state of Utah. Here are some of them.

Sports: Golden Circle Marathon (Blanding), Utah Summer Games (Cedar City), Rodeos and horse races (Cedar City), Cutter, snowmobile, and dog sled races (Heber City), Rodeo (Kanab), Rod Run and Chili Cook-Off (Lake Powell), Steam Threshing Bee (Logan), Canyonlands Festival and Rodeo (Moab), Winter Sun Run-10K Race (Moab), Canyonlands PRCA Rodeo/Butch Cassidy Days (Moab), Pioneer Days Rodeo (Ogden), Horse racing (Panguitch), Snow Sculpture Contest (Park City), Ride and Tie (Park City), Showdown Classic/Jeremy Ranch (Park City), Drag Races/Dixie Raceway (St. George), Dinosaur Roundup Rodeo (Vernal), Water Skiing Competition (Vernal), Bonneville National Speed Trials (Wendover), Western Stampede (West Jordan).

Arts and Crafts: Utah Pageant of the Arts (American Fork), Bluff Indian Day (Bluff), Peach Day Celebration (Brigham City), Rock, Gem and Mineral Show (Moab), Art Festival (Park City), Utah Arts Festival (Salt Lake City), National Quilt Show (Springville).

Music: American Folk Ballet Summer Festival (Cedar City), Utah Symphony Pops Concert (Ogden), Temple Square Christmas (Salt Lake City), Utah Opera Company (Salt Lake City), Ballet West (Salt Lake City), Ririe-Woodbury Dance Company (Salt Lake City), Repertory Dance Theatre (Salt Lake City), Utah Symphony (Salt

Lake City), Utah Symphony (Snowbird).

Entertainment: New Year's Eve Torchlight Parade and Fireworks (Brian Head), Driving of Golden Spike (Brigham City), Railroaders Festival (Brigham City), Highland Heritage Festival (Cedar City), Midsummer Renaissance Faire (Cedar City), Tintic-Silver Festival (Eureka), Melon Days (Green River), Friendship Cruise (Green River), Wasatch County Fair (Heber City), Swiss Days (Heber City), Desert Vagabond Days (Kanab), Festival of the American West (Logan), Cache County Fair (Logan), Swiss Christmas (Midway), Jeep Safari (Moab), Friendship Cruise (Moab), Monticello Pioneer Days (Monticello), San Juan County 4-H Fair (Monticello), National Western Film Festival (Ogden), Winter Fest (Ogden), Miner's Day Celebration (Park City), United States Film Festival (Park City), Autumn Aloft Hot Air Balloon Festival (Park City), Salmon supper (Payson), Golden Onion Days (Payson), Freedom Festival (Provo), Washington County Fair (St. George), Dixie Roundup (St. George), Pioneer Christmas Days (Salt Lake City), Utah State Fair (Salt Lake City), Day's of '47 Celebration (Salt Lake City), World Folkfest

Two children enjoy themselves at the Park City Art Festival.

A performance of the Utah Opera Company of Salt Lake City.

A lone cowboy participates in this section of the Rodeo Days of '47.

(Springville), Outlaw Trail Festival (Vernal), Southern Utah Folklife Festival (Zion National Park).

Tours: Jeep Jamboree (Blanding), Guided Pack Trips and Mountain Trail Rides

(Kamas), Wagons West (St. George).

Theater: Utah Shakespearian Festival (Cedar City), Shakespeare Festival (Park City), Egyptian Theatre (Park City), Pageant of the Arts (Provo),

Pioneer Players (St. George), Mormon Miracle Pageant (Salina), Pioneer Memorial Theatre (Salt Lake City), The "Promised Valley" (Salt Lake City), Utah Arts Festival (Salt Lake City).

Famous People

Many famous people were born in the state of Utah. Here are a few:

Maude Adams 1872-1953, Salt Lake City. Stage actress

Florence E. Allen 1884-1966, Salt Lake City. First woman appointed to a U.S. court of appeals

Solon Hannibal Borglum 1868-1922, Ogden. Sculptor

Frank Borzage 1893-1962, Salt Lake City. Film director

John Moses Browning 1855-1926, Ogden. Firearms designer

Virgil Carter b. 1945, Anabella. Football quarterback

Tom Chambers b. 1959, Ogden. Basketball player

Joshua R. Clark, Jr. 1871-1961, Grantsville. Lawyer, diplomat and churchman

Cyrus E. Dallin 1861-1944, Springville. Sculptor

Laraine Day b. 1917, Roosevelt. Film actress: *The Locket, The Third Voice*

Bernard De Voto 1897-1955, Ogden. Pulitzer Prize-winning historian

Kelly Downs b. 1960, Ogden. Baseball pitcher

Marriner S. Eccles 1890-1977, Logan. Financier

Philo T. Farnsworth 1906-71, Beaver. Inventor of electronic devices that led to the invention of television

Maude Adams reached the height of her career in 1905 as the lead in the play Peter Pan.

Bernard De Voto received a Pulitzer Prize in 1947 for his book Across the Wide Mississippi.

Herman Franks b. 1914, Price. Baseball manager

Gene Fullmer b. 1931, West Jordan. Middleweight boxing champion

John Gilbert 1895-1936, Logan. Silent film actor: *Love, Queen Christina*

William D. Haywood 1869-1928, Salt Lake City. Labor organizer

John Held, Jr. 1889-1958, Salt Lake City. Cartoonist and

David McKay was the ninth president (1951-70) of the Mormon church. The membership in the church increased from 1.1 to 2.9 million in the 19 years of McKay's leadership.

illustrator

Frank T. Hines 1879-1960, Salt Lake City. Army officer and government official

Bruce Hurst b. 1958, St. George. Baseball pitcher

Florence P. Kahn 1866-1948, Salt Lake City. Congresswoman

Goodwin J. Knight 1896-1970, Provo. Governor of California

David O. McKay 1873-1970, Huntsville. President of the Church of Jesus Christ of Latter-Day Saints

Dick Motta b. 1931, Salt Lake City. Professional basketball coach

Red Nichols 1905-65, Ogden. Jazz trumpeter and bandleader

Merlin Olsen b. 1940, Logan. Hall of Fame football player

Donny Osmond b. 1957, Ogden. Pop singer

Marie Osmond b. 1959, Ogden. Pop singer

Ivy Baker Priest 1905-75, Kimberley. U.S. Treasurer

Dick Romney 1895-1969, Salt Lake City. College football coach

Byron Scott b. 1961, Ogden. Basketball player

George Albert Smith 1870-1951, Salt Lake City. President of the Church of Jesus Christ of Latter-day Saints

Reed O. Smoot 1862-1941, Salt Lake City. Senate leader

Virginia Sorensen b. 1912, Provo. Novelist: *A Little Lower than the Angels, The Neighbors*

Elbert D. Thomas 1883-1953, Salt Lake City. Senate leader

Robert Walker 1914-51, Salt Lake City. Film actor: *One Touch of Venus, Strangers on a Train*

Ervin Wardman 1865-1923, Salt Lake City. Journalist

Loretta Young b. 1913, Salt Lake City. Academy Award-winning actress: *The Farmer's Daughter, Come to the Stable*

Mahonri M. Young 1877-1957, Salt Lake City. Sculptor

Colleges and Universities

There are several colleges and universities in Utah. Here are the more prominent, with their locations, dates of founding, and enrollments.

Brigham Young University,
Provo, 1875, 27,973

Southern Utah State College,
Cedar City, 1897, 3,629

University of Utah, Salt Lake
City, 1850, 23,626

Utah State University, Logan,
1888, 12,650

Weber State College, Ogden,
1889, 12,920

*Westminster College of Salt
Lake City,* Salt Lake City,
1875, 1,977

**Where To Get More
Information**
Utah Travel Council
Council Hall
Capitol Hill
Salt Lake City UT 84114
Or call 1-801-538-1030

Bibliography

General

Aylesworth, Thomas G. and Virginia L. Aylesworth. *Let's Discover the States: The West.* New York: Chelsea House, 1988.

Arizona

Arizona, A Guide to the Grand Canyon State. New York: Hastings House, 1940.

Carpenter, Allan. *Arizona,* rev. ed. Chicago: Childrens Press, 1979.

Chanin, Abe and Mildred Chanin. *This Land, These Voices: A Different View of Arizona History in the Words of Those Who Lived It.* Flagstaff, AZ: Northland Press, 1977.

Fradin, Dennis B. *Arizona in Words and Pictures.* Chicago: Childrens Press, 1980.

Love, Frank. *Arizona's Story: A Short History.* New York: Norton, 1979.

Miller, Joseph. *Arizona; The Grand Canyon State; A State Guide,* rev. ed. New York: Hastings House, 1966.

Powell, Lawrence Clark.

Arizona: A Bicentennial History. New York: Norton, 1977.

Sloan, Richard E., and Ward R. Adams. *History of Arizona.* 4 vols. Phoenix, Arizona: Record Publishing Company, 1930.

Trimble, Marshall. *Arizona: A Panoramic History of a Frontier State.* Garden City, NY: Doubleday, 1977.

Nevada

Angel, Myron, ed. *History of Nevada.* New York: Arno Press, 1973.

Carpenter, Allan. *Nevada,* rev. ed. Chicago: Childrens Press, 1979.

Davis, Samuel P. *The History of Nevada.* 2 vols. Las Vegas, NV: Nevada Publications, 1984.

Elliott, Russell R. *History of Nevada.* Lincoln, NE: University of Nebraska Press, 1973.

Fradin, Dennis B. *Nevada in Words and Pictures.* Chicago: Childrens Press, 1981.

Hulse, James W. *The Nevada Adventure: A History,* 5th ed.

Reno, NV: University of Nevada Press, 1981.

Laxalt, Robert. *Nevada: A Bicentennial History.* New York: Norton, 1977.

Lillard, Richard G. *Desert Challenge: An Interpretation of Nevada.* Westport, CT: Greenwood, 1979.

Utah

Carpenter, Allan. *Utah,* rev. ed. Chicago: Childrens Press, 1979.

Deseret, 1776-1976: A Bicentennial Illustrated History of Utah, by the Deseret News. Salt Lake City, UT: Deseret News Press, 1975.

Fradin, Dennis B. *Utah in Words and Pictures.* Chicago: Childrens Press, 1980.

Luce, Willard and Celia Luce. *Utah!* Layton, UT: Peregrine Smith, 1975.

Peterson, Charles S. *Utah, A History.* New York: Norton, 1984.

Poll, Richard D., and others, eds. *Utah's History.* Provo, UT: Brigham Young University Press, 1978.

Photo Credits/Acknowledgments

Photos on pages 3 (top), 5, courtesy of Arizona Secretary of State; pages 7, 9, 10-14, 16-22, Arizona Office of Tourism; pages 3 (middle), 25-27, 29-30, 33-39, courtesy of Nevada Commission on Tourism; pages 3 (bottom), 41, 43, 46-48, courtesy of Utah Travel Council; pages 45, 49-52, 54-55, 57-58, 61, courtesy of Salt Lake Convention and Visitors Bureau; pages 6-7, 53, courtesy of National Park Service; pages 42-43, 56-57, courtesy of Park City Chamber/Bureau; pages 6-7, Woodbridge Williams; pages 31-32, courtesy of Nevada Magazine/Caroline Joy Hadley; page 15, courtesy of City of Phoenix Public Information Office/Bob Rink; page 23, courtesy of New York Public Library; page 24, courtesy of Office of Morris Udall; page 40, courtesy of The Paul Laxalt Group; pages 42-43, Hughes Martin; page 47, Scott T. Smith; page 48, Frank Jensen; page 53, Margaret Farrell; page 59, courtesy of Utah Historical Society; page 60, courtesy of Church of Jesus Christ of Latter-Day Saints.

Cover photograph courtesy of Arizona Office of Tourism.